FIND OUT WHO'S NORMAL AND WHO'S NOT

FIND OUT WHO'S NORMAL AND WHO'S NOT

The Proven System to Quickly Assess Anyone's Emotional Stability

David J. Lieberman, Ph.D.

Viter Press New Jersey

VITER PRESS

Publisher's Cataloging-In-Publication Data
(Prepared by The Donohue Group, Inc.)

Lieberman, David J.,
    Find out who's normal and who's not: the proven system to quickly assess anyone's emotional stability / David J. Lieberman.

    p. cm.

    Includes bibliographical references.
    ISBN-13: 978-0-9786313-2-1
    ISBN-10: 0-9786313-2-3

1. Personality assessment--Popular works. 2. Prediction (Psychology)--Popular works. 3. Personality disorders--Popular works. I. Title.

BF698 .L54 2009
155.28   2009929475

CONTENTS

Note to Readers

This book is not designed to be used as a diagnostic tool or a substitute for psychotherapy or any other treatment. Rather, it's meant to be used as a guide for evaluating a person's general emotional health. If you believe that you, or anyone you know, may be in danger of harming themselves or others, please seek help immediately from the appropriate authorities or mental health professionals.

INTRODUCTION

We all know the relatively harmless neighborhood character who treats his front lawn like a battlefield, choosing to communicate his boundaries to rambunctious neighborhood children by positioning "Keep off the Grass" signs like a squadron of land mines. Is this person capable of hurting anyone? Doubtful. But would we invite him over for dinner? Not anytime soon. Likewise, we're probably not likely to extend a job offer to the scruffy guy who stands on the street corner every day waving a "The World is Ending Tomorrow" sign.

But what about the new plumber, who thirty minutes into the job, decides to open the refrigerator and help himself to a beverage? Or the convenience store cashier we barely know who has the audacity to reach over and drop our purchase into our open purse? He gazes at us defiantly, daring us to say something . . . is he potentially dangerous? If so, to what extent?

The cosmos of emotional solvency can be a gray and murky terrain. Sometimes behaviors that seem innocent or even kindly at first glance are, in fact, red flags signaling us that something is wrong.

There are always people lurking at the periphery of our lives (or even closer) whose lack of emotional stability can, and often does, affect us. Maybe they wouldn't walk into a school with a gun and a backpack full of ammunition, but that doesn't mean we want them taking care of our children, dating our daughters, or managing our money.

The world we inhabit is very different from the one our grandparents occupied; it is slowly but surely evolving into a world without borders. Technological advancements are transforming the way we communicate with others, redefining or erasing old boundaries. We're constantly meeting new people, whether virtually or face-to-face; nowadays we have the capability to conduct business with people on the other side of the planet as seamlessly as if they were sitting in the same room with us.

Often, we don't have time—or don't *take* time—to learn what we really need to know about those who we associate with. Yet, assessing the emotional health of the people in our lives has never been more important, even if they're just passing through. While many of our interactions are fleeting and benign—such as encounters with a waitress or a delivery man — others may develop into long-lasting friendships or lifelong relationships.

And not everyone is as healthy and emotionally stable as they may seem. It's an unfortunate reality that cannot be ignored. You've probably had the experience of making a new friend or acquaintance, only to discover in the ensuing months that something is off about that person. What might appear at the beginning to be just a harmless quirk could in actual fact be something more disturbing. You're left wishing that if only you had observed the warning signs from the outset, you would have never become involved with this person.

When we allow an individual into our lives—whether it is in a professional or personal capacity—we are placing our trust in them, and as such, are making a decision that can potentially have profound and far-reaching consequences.

If you are concerned about a new relationship, or even an old one, you will no longer need to rely on instincts, hunches, or horoscopes. This book will provide you with tools to assemble a psychological snapshot of almost any individual, starting from day one.

The purpose of *Find Out Who's Normal and Who's Not* is to help you learn to protect yourself and your loved ones— emotionally, financially, and physically—from unstable individuals who will inevitably pass through your life, bearing in mind that the observed may in fact be more stable than the observer.

Note:

Throughout this book the pronouns he and she are used interchangeably. This does not indicate that one gender is more likely to be suffering from a certain illness or effect (except where noted).

SECTION 1

Human Nature

CHAPTER 1

The Psyche Unleashed

Whoever doesn't know it
must learn and find by experience
that a quiet conscience makes one strong.

ANNE FRANK

I n order to be happy, maintain good relationships, and achieve emotional wellbeing, we have to feel good about ourselves (Cheng & Furnham, 2004). This means that we need to literally love ourselves; this self-love is called self-esteem.

Where Does Self-esteem Come From?

Within each of us exist three inner forces: the *body*, the *ego*, and the *soul*. These forces are often at odds with each other.

Briefly, the body wants to do what *feels* good; the ego wants to do what *looks* good; and the soul wants to do what *is* good.

Doing what's easy or comfortable is a body drive. The body drive can encourage us to overindulge our cravings or desires (such as overeating or oversleeping). We allow ourselves to gratify our desires, even though we know better, purely because of how it *feels*.

An ego drive can run the gamut from making a joke at someone else's expense to buying a flashy car that we can't afford. When we're motivated by ego, we do things that we believe project our desired image of ourselves. These choices are not based on what *is* good, but on what makes us *look* good. (When the ego is engaged, it deceives us in four primary ways: (1) It chooses that on which we focus; (2) it makes what we see all about us; (3) it concludes that all negative experiences are due to a deficiency within ourselves — albeit often unconsciously; (4) it causes us to believe that we can think our way out of a situation that is beyond our control.)

If we can't control our behaviors, seek immediate gratification, or strive to keep up an image, we become angry with ourselves, and consequently feel empty inside. Our self-esteem and self-respect are eroded. To compensate for these feelings of guilt and inadequacy, the ego engages — we become self-focused, or *egocentric*.

We only gain self-esteem when we're able to make

responsible choices and do what's right, regardless of what we *feel like doing*, or how it appears to others. This is the soul-driven (moral or conscience) choice that elevates us to the higher altitude of healthy perspective. Self-esteem and the ego are inversely related, like a seesaw: when one goes up, the other goes down.

In every situation, we utilize both our emotional and intellectual selves. When we view the world from an emotional perspective, we contort our thinking and rationale to justify our emotional attitudes, beliefs, and actions. In effect, we place the full weight and force of our convictions behind an illogical conclusion. The lower our self-esteem, the less objective we are. Our perspective is child-like and narrow, resulting in an excessive focus on the here-and-now rather than the big picture.

Imagine that a little girl is playing with her doll and her brother suddenly snatches it away — she feels as if her whole world has been turned upside down. This is how low self-esteem manifests itself in adults; we lose sight of the big picture.

When, however, we approach a situation with objectivity and clarity, we can draw on our emotions, rather than allowing our emotions to reign over us; we become impassioned and drive our more rational thinking with productive passion and enthusiasm.

What Is the Source of Conflict?

As human beings, we are hardwired to like ourselves, but when we aren't able to nourish ourselves though good choices and self-respect, we turn to the rest of the world to feed us.

Self-esteem and ego both pivot on respect. We must get respect from somewhere, and if we can't get it from ourselves, we demand it from others. We become emotional terrorists, manipulative and needy; some of us get what we want with honey, others with vinegar. Regardless of the method, we essentially hold others hostage until they give us the emotional nourishment we crave. (We must be unambiguous, here. This behavior is rarely consciously examined. Few people wake up in the morning with the thought: *How can I make someone's life miserable.* While we are all responsible for our behavior, we must not assume a malicious intent. When we suffer from low self-esteem we are literally driven by an instinctive craving for love and recognition.)

Those of us with low self-esteem believe that if only others would care enough about us, we could convert their adoration and praise to self-love. Unlike the energy our bodies receive from eating natural foods, this verbal ransom is emotional junk food. Empty and unsatisfying, it doesn't provide us with the nutrition we really need.

We are never truly contented, even when the reinforcement we get from others is positive; when we do not love ourselves, we cannot truly feel the love of others. Consequently, we sabotage relationships.

To illustrate the point, imagine pouring water into a cup that has no bottom. As someone pours in the water, the cup feels and looks full. As long as the cup is constantly being filled, we are satisfied. But the minute someone stops filling it (with undivided attention, respect, or adoration), the cup quickly becomes empty and we are left as thirsty as ever. A bottomless cup will never be full; and our thirst can never be quenched, no matter how much we receive. We experience fleeting contentment, but we lack a solid vessel to contain it. It flows out just as rapidly as it flowed in. Ultimately, we remain empty inside.

King Solomon, the wisest of men, writes, "A lacking on the inside can never be satisfied with something from the outside." People who seek self-esteem from external sources can never be truly content. They are the very epitome of a bottomless pit.

When we lack self-esteem, we will seek praise from anyone and feel inferior to everyone, regardless of the source's credibility; we'll even seek reinforcement from total strangers. Interestingly enough, although we can feel offended by anyone, we may feel particularly hurt when we feel disrespected by someone who is smart, wealthy, or attractive. We unconsciously assign a higher value to people with any of those attributes, and their words and deeds have an especially devastating impact on our fragile self-esteem.

When we're at the mercy of others for proof of our worth, we become anxious, vulnerable, and insecure. We overanalyze and overreact to every fleeting glance or passing comment.

But when we enjoy high self-esteem, we tend not to dissect or take offense at meaningless and insignificant comments made during casual conversation. A mature, adult perspective allows us to consider whether perhaps the person who offended us suffers from low self-esteem and has his own hang-ups and issues. We don't automatically assume that his words or actions imply disrespect. And even if we do ultimately conclude that he doesn't respect us, we are not angry as a result. High self-esteem means that we don't need someone else's respect in order to respect ourselves.

Scared People Behave Badly

When we get angry, it is because we are, to some degree, fearful. We are fearful because we have lost control over a certain aspect of our life — our circumstances, understanding of the world, or our self-image. The response to fear — the ego's attempt to compensate for this perceived loss — is anger. Fear is the root of all negative emotions — envy, lust, jealousy, and especially anger. When we feel threatened, we go into defense mode. Anger fortifies the ego and allows us to operate under the illusion that we are in control. At the root of fear is low self-esteem. This explains why angry people have low self-esteem, are argumentative, stubborn, and quick to flare up yet slow to forgive. Those behaviors are defenses against the underlying fear.

Low self-esteem causes us to constantly question our own self-worth; and we become highly sensitive to how others treat us. Our opinion of ourselves fluctuates with our perceived ability to impress others, so when someone is rude to us, embarrasses us, or treats us with disrespect, we may be quick to lash out in anger.

Not everyone, however, allows anger to take control of their lives or wields it so obviously. People respond to conflict in one of four ways:

- Accept
- Retreat
- Surrender
- Fight

Acceptance is the healthiest response. The person who accepts the situation doesn't become angry or allow his emotions to dictate his response.

Retreat is typical of passive-aggressive individuals, who withdraw or retreat in order to avoid confrontation. The passive-aggressive person lacks the self-esteem to face the situation head on, so he backs down in the moment, but gets back at the person in another way, at another time. His retaliation, or revenge, may take the form of being late, "forgetting" to do something important for the other, or just generally inconveniencing her in some way.

The person who **surrenders** simply gives up and gives in, a response that often produces codependency and a doormat or compliant personality type. He doesn't feel worthy enough to stand up for himself and/or feels he is incapable of advancing his own agenda, needs, and wishes.

The fourth potential response, **fighting**, produces direct and unhealthy conflict. This person is emotionally charged and enraged, and chooses to battle it out.

Indeed, low self-esteem can trigger a powerful unconscious desire to mistreat those who care about us. The less self-control we have, the more desperate we are to control or manipulate the events and people around us, especially those closest to us. Because self-control leads to self-respect, we need to feel as if we are in control of someone or something—anything.

It's About Choice

Our overall level of self-control is the primary barometer which determines how annoyed, frustrated, or angered we become in any given situation. Self-control gives us the capacity to make better choices—which increases our self-esteem and thus shrinks the ego—as well as the emotional perspective to see the world objectively and clearly.

Although people experience strong emotional reactions to major changes in their lives, those reactions tend to subside rapidly. For example, studies show that big lottery winners often lead miserable lives after their windfall. After an initial period of adjustment, they're generally not much happier than they were before their big win. Some are even quite miserable, despite their newfound wealth. (Equally compelling, this same study revealed that recent paraplegics were themselves not much unhappier—after a six-month readjustment period—than the control group [Brickman, Coates & Janoff-Bulman, 1978]).

A statistically disproportionate number of suicides, murders, drunk-driving arrests, divorces, and even bankruptcies befall these lottery winners, a phenomenon that has been dubbed the "lottery curse." We might find it perplexing that such misfortune would fall on such fortunate souls. After all, if someone took a poll, asking: "If you won $100 million dollars in tonight's lottery, would you be happy for the rest of your life?" most of us would respond with a resounding *Yes!*

But here's the fallacy . . .

Since, to a great extent, positive self-esteem comes from making good choices, instant money or fame can fuel even greater destructive behaviors and more drastic overindulgences for people who are not accustomed to exercising self-control.

Of course, the impact of external circumstances on our mood fluctuates. We all have our bad days and good days. But true emotional stability remains fairly constant, regardless of our daily trials and tribulations. It is the power of free will, and the subsequent choices we make, that ultimately shape the quality of our emotional lives.

Whether it is from the media, or from our own personal experience, we have all heard of people who have led charmed upbringings, yet a succession of stunningly irresponsible choices led them down a path of misery. But we also know people who have been dealt one challenge after another, yet soared above even the most daunting situations and heartaches, embracing their futures with optimistic resolve.

It's Not What We Have, It's What We Do With What We Have

The research is clear. With regards to income, physical attractiveness (Diener & Wolsic and Fujita, 1995) and intelligence (Diener, 1984; Emmons & Diener, 1985) each has been shown to have little effect on our overall emotional wellbeing.

Even our physical health has been shown to play a nonexistent or negligible role in our emotional health. The converse, however, is not true; our emotional issues drastically affect our physical health. (When objective health is examined by a physician's ratings, the correlation between physical and the emotional health weakens considerably. In some cases it even disappears [Watten, Vassend, Myhrer, & Syversen, 1997]).

While psychological or emotional problems may be classified under the broad umbrella of mental health disorders, they can take a tremendous toll on our physical health.

Ultimately, there is no such thing as a mind-body split. Our mental and physical states are inextricably bound. Psychological symptoms have just as much impact on our health as physical symptoms.

Psychological disorders, in fact, typically present with both psychological (mind and emotions) and somatic (biological and physiological) symptoms. For example, people who suffer from clinical depression often exhibit somatic symptoms such as insomnia, fatigue and loss of energy, appetite changes, significant weight gain or loss, and psychomotor changes (e.g. slower motor movements or faster, agitated movements).

To be abundantly clear, while the choices we make throughout our lives have a profound impact on our emotional stability, mental health disorders result from a combination of factors — genes, neurochemistry, environmental stressors, childhood traumas, and other developmental factors (see Chapter 13, "Family Ties: Is It All in the Genes?"). And although there is no discounting the power of exercising our free will and its influence on every aspect of our lives, a person's emotional instability may be partly attributed (or in atypical cases, even entirely) to aspects beyond his control.

The Path to Self-Destruction

There is a direct correlation between self-contempt and self-inflicted punishment that comes in the disguise of pleasurable indulgences. Self-destructive behaviors such as excessive eating, alcohol abuse, drug use, and gambling are nothing more than distractions that help us avoid having to examine our lives — ourselves — too closely.

We long to feel good about who we are, to truly love ourselves. But without self-esteem — without self-love — we end up losing ourselves. If we feel worthless, we are incapable of investing in our own wellbeing and happiness. Instead, we seek out indulgences that will feed our empty selves, and help us escape from our pain. Studies conclusively show the link between low self-esteem levels and a range of self-destructive behaviors and habits, including compulsive shopping (Lee, 1999), binge drinking (Bladt, 2002), and binge eating (Tassava, 2001).

Avoiding pain through overindulgence is a cruel cycle, and sooner or later it will spiral out of control. When we don't feel good about ourselves, we seek the temporary and hollow refuge of immediate gratification. We surrender to our impulses rather than rise above them. We look for a quick fix, rather than a lasting solution to the pain and hollowness we feel inside. The passing comfort and feeling of security quickly dissipates, and we find ourselves in even greater discomfort.

Overindulgence is not coping. It's avoidance. Denial ultimately robs us of emotional, physical, and spiritual health, and all but guarantees that we will continue to struggle to find peace, purpose, and contentment.

It is easier to avoid pain than it used to be. In days of old, we were inclined to make better choices because the consequences of our poor judgments were more immediate, and trickier to conceal. But today, there are far more means of escapism at our disposal, allowing us to blithely ignore our problems and the reality of our situation.

These days, we probably wouldn't even be startled to see an emphysema sufferer rolling around with an oxygen tank strapped to his wheelchair, chain-smoking cigarettes. One would think he would have gotten the message about the risks of smoking, not to mention the new, additional risk of combustion.

Thanks to technology and 21st-century medical advances, we have more toys, tools, and excuses than ever from which to concoct elaborate avoidances. Technology — arguably an addiction in itself — has become a popular enabler, the new Great Escape. Computers, televisions, smartphones . . . everywhere we turn, there are convenient vehicles for mindless distraction.

Instant shrink-wrapped entertainment offers escape into other worlds, a never-ending labyrinth of video games, movies, TV shows, blogs, and forums where we'll find others just like us. With the touch of a button or a click of a mouse we can dissociate from the pain *du jour*, thus seemingly avoiding the repercussions of the poor choices we have made, and continue to make, in our lives.

We no longer have to worry about being alone with our thoughts. Thinking, after all, is what gets us into trouble in the first place. Thinking leads to feeling, and feeling doesn't always feel good.

We need to be distracted, to be taken away from ourselves. We're afraid to be alone with our own thoughts, so we seek outside distractions to block out the noise coming from within. The constant chatter of the mind, the worries, fears, and anxieties cannot be turned off, so we attempt to tune out.

Don't Think, Take a Pill

Not only do we avoid pain at all costs, we are no longer willing to even endure discomfort. Feeling a little stiff? Down a couple of Ibuprofen. Suffering indigestion because we ate more than our body can metabolize? Take an antacid. Lactose intolerant? Take Lactaid.

If we ingest too much of the wrong thing, don't worry. There are laxatives for constipation. Antidiarrheals for diarrhea. Aspirin for headaches. And calcium carbonate hangover prevention supplements to nip those hangovers in the bud.

But uh-oh, now we're experiencing serious side effects? Don't worry, there's always a pill chase. Just take another pill to counteract the negative side effects of the first pill. Ibuprofen causing ulcers? Pop a few Zantac. Gastric bypass procedure causing blood clots in our legs? Unstaple that stomach and hook up the old plumbing. But what happens when the parts on the old jalopy are shot because we drank too much alcohol and ingested a glutinous excess of trans fatty foods? Not to worry. Before the body shuts down altogether, we can simply wangle a slot on the liver and heart transplant lists and replace the defective parts.

It's true that our modern fixes rewire our systems, but they also open the door to rampant abuse. We have come to expect that no matter how much damage we inflict on ourselves, there will always be something or somebody who will rescue us. And even if there's no remedy today, there will be one just around the corner, or so we've become conditioned to believe.

And what about our emotional wellbeing?

The media helpfully keeps us abreast of new advances that

promise to make our lives more fun. Not to mention their sponsors. It's virtually impossible to turn on the TV these days without catching a pharma-commercial that promises to cure whatever ails us. *If you or someone you know is suffering from Disease XYZ . . . Ask your doctor if Drug X is right for you . . .*

Every day we're bombarded with imagery promising nirvana . . . Serene little butterflies flying through our bedrooms at night, presiding over our restful night's sleep. Newlyweds gazing at each other adoringly as the wedding party looks on, showering the happy couple with rice—and all because the bride is herself again.

We Cannot Beat the System

The system — the human mind and body — is rigged to revolt against negligence, abuse, and indifference. One-fourth of all adults suffer from some form of mental illness. Depression alone is killing us, and it can be integrally linked to pain avoidance behaviors. According to the National Institute of Mental Health, as much as 16 percent of the US population (35 million people) suffers from clinical depression.

The system will faithfully keep dishing out new symptoms, each more grave than the last, to remind us that we haven't still addressed the root problem. Even if we don't pay an immediate price for our overindulgent ways, the natural recursions and endless loops multiply damage in geometric progression. Interest may be deferred, but that balloon payment will come due sooner or later.

Mask it, conceal, it, dilute it — the pain doesn't go away. Overindulgence is not coping. It's avoidance. Regaining control of our behavior, on our own or with professional help, is the only way to regain control of our lives. Altering the thought patterns that provoke self-damaging behaviors enable us to repair what has been broken.

◆ ◆ ◆

Emotions, thoughts, and feelings, after all, are not tangible, but they leave footprints, visible clues. The skilled profiler can assess a person's emotional health in much the same way that a trained physician can give a patient a once-over and determine, with a degree of reliability, the general physical health of the individual — or at least know to a reasonable degree of certainty whether or not the person is seriously ill. It is imperative however, that a psychological profiler understand that his own bias can color his perception. This is known as *diagnostic bias.*

CHAPTER 2

Diagnosis Bias:
The System as We Know It

The only thing that interferes with my learning is my education.
ALBERT EINSTEIN

How do criminal profilers construct profiles of serial kill-ers they've never met? How do doctors arrange symptoms into a diagnosis for a new patient? Both rely on problem-solving strategies and mental shortcuts to find solutions more effi-ciently. However, mental shortcuts can also feed our cognitive biases and encourage us to jump to false conclusions. In fact, we sometimes end up jumping to the same false conclusion again and again.

Cognitive biases lead to thinking errors which impede

our ability to make objective diagnoses. Biases often occur unconsciously, outside the realm of self-knowledge or introspection, and leak into our judgments — even when the bias stands in opposition to our conscious beliefs.

We all have natural biases; one of our strongest, for example, is our tendency to try to connect random events that happen to occur together, and blame one for causing the other.

The phenomenon of cognitive biases helps explain why we tend to find whatever it is we're looking for. Expressed differently, we tend to see what we expect to see because we turn a blind eye to any evidence that doesn't conform to our expectations. When a cognitive bias is at work, the evidence seems — almost mystically — to arrange itself into patterns and concepts which we then sort into categories and label accordingly.

That is not to say that biases are negative. A bias is part of the neurobiological process by which the brain constructs categories and concepts. It's a shortcut, and often serves us well. After all, we solve problems all day, every day. Imagine if we had to start from scratch on every single problem — from how to operate the coffee maker to finding the fastest way to get to work. We'd never get anything done.

Categories are the building blocks of thinking and decision-making. The brain loves categories, but it can be lazy about how it uses them. It prefers to cram new information into existing categories rather than build new ones. The brain is always on the lookout for similarities between people, objects, or experiences, hoping to treat new information as data which will neatly and readily fit into one of our familiar, remembered groups.

There are two schools of thought on how we form concepts: the critical features theory and the prototype hypothesis. Critical features theory holds that the brain stores lists of the critical characteristics that define concepts. A concept is a member of the category if (and only if) it has every feature on the list. For example, critical features for the concept of fish would be gills and fins.

But what about jellyfish? It has no gills or fins, yet is labeled *jellyfish*. The critical features approach, as we can see, is extremely rigid. The prototype approach is slightly more flexible. It allows us to build a mental model of the ideal or representative characteristics that category members should have, but a person, object, or situation doesn't have to exactly match all the features of the prototype in order to be included in the category.

The American Psychiatric Association's Diagnostic and Statistical Manual of Mental Disorders (DSM-IV-TR), which is the therapist's go-to guide for classifying mental illnesses, might be thought of as a catalog of mental health prototypes. The DSM formally sorts diagnostic criteria into categories — disorders — and labels them.

How Biases Develop

We can trace the roots of bias to our problem-solving strategies. Two strategies, for example, that help us solve complex problems are algorithms and heuristics. An algorithmic approach involves systematically thinking through every possible solution or explanation, while the heuristic approach uses more generalized rule-of-thumb strategies that have worked for us in similar past situations.

Algorithms, obviously, involve more work and take more time to implement than heuristics. So we often rely on heuristics — shortcuts — to help us solve a puzzle. Heuristics can be useful for helping us solve problems efficiently, but they can lead to biases which cause us to slip into a guilty until proven innocent, problem-solving mode.

We use availability heuristics to estimate probabilities; if we've experienced a situation before, we're likely to overestimate the frequency of its occurrence. For example, if a detective investigating a woman's murder knows that the majority of the murders he has investigated were committed by the spouse, he might be more likely to jump to the conclusion that the husband did it and begin to mentally arrange evidence to support his theory. But the murderer might turn out to be the next door neighbor, or some random person who just happened to wander into the neighborhood and had no previous connection to the murder victim. This is not to say that statistics are not a highly useful tool (as we will see in Chapter 11, "Statistically Speaking"), but the mistake lies in giving them exclusive, rather than proportional, weight.

If a doctor frequently treats people with depression, he might be more inclined to hear a patient's complaint of symptoms, such as fatigue, energy loss, weight gain, and decreased libido, and conclude that the person suffers from depression. But the problem could also be hypothyroidism, or fifty other maladies which manifest themselves in similar symptoms.

We also tend to fall back on representativeness heuristics, in which we group people into categories. Once we're categorized, it's assumed that we share all the features of other members in our category, and they share ours. If we have a preconceived notion about a particular group, we may jump to conclusions about individual members of that group, while stubbornly ignoring evidence that refutes our conclusion.

You Get What You Expect

Biases create expectations; we develop schemas or blueprints that help us anticipate what we'll find when we encounter a particular concept, category, person, or situation. If, for example, a physician's schema for Attention-Deficit Disorder (AD/HD) includes an expectation that people who show symptoms of hyperactivity must have AD/HD, he will be prone to frequent misdiagnosis of the condition. Not all people who are hyperactive have AD/HD and not all people who have AD/HD are hyperactive.

Schemas help us fill in blanks quickly. Unfortunately, schemas are biased by our experiences, and they can nudge us to fill in some of those blanks with the wrong answers. If we approach new information with a preconceived notion of how it's supposed to fit into our grand schema, we may retain information that conforms to our expectations and discard information that doesn't.

The ripple effect is what can be most devastating because it engages the impact of expectation within ourselves.

The Law of Expectancy predicts that we will tend to live up to what is expected of us. Numerous studies demonstrate the powerful role that expectation plays in comprehension and execution, and include such findings as: (a) girls who were told that they would perform poorly on a math test did so (Becker, 1981); (b) assembly line workers who were told that the job was complex and difficult performed less efficiently at the same task than those who were told that it was easy and simple (Rosenthal, 1976); and (c) adults who were given fairly complex mazes solved them faster when told that they were based on a grade-school level (Jussim & Harber, 2005).

When an expert or authority figure diagnoses or labels us, we tend to take on the characteristics associated with the label, for better or for worse. In the world of clinical diagnosis, this phenomenon tends to manifest as the dark side of the Pygmalion effect, sometimes referred to as the Golem effect. In other words, the diagnosis itself can cause us to take on those negative traits and behaviors.

A *diagnosis*, in the end, is nothing more than a cluster of symptoms. A *person* is so much more than that. The person is not the illness, and the illness is not the person.

Developing an awareness of our own biases allows us to draw more objective and more accurate conclusions about the behaviors of others. Two other major types of bias exist: personality and culture.

Every Hammer Sees a Nail

The clinician's own personality can hamper his ability to accurately assess a psychological disorder. In one study of primary care physicians, they were characterized along three dimensions: dutifulness (conscientiousness), vulnerability (anxiousness), and openness to feelings (empathy). Dutiful/conscientious doctors were more likely to explore and document a patient's psychosocial and life circumstances, but asked fewer questions — perhaps due to concerns about time-economy or a reluctance to broach sensitive topics such as depression or suicide.

Anxious/vulnerable doctors were also more likely to thoroughly document a depression diagnosis, but involve the patient less. Highly empathetic doctors with average — as opposed to extremely high — levels of conscientiousness were most likely to be trusted by patients (Duberstein, 2008).

Culture Bias

Culture influences our mental schemas and shapes our personalities — from parenting strategies and the values we instill to the social and religious rituals we practice. Social norms within a culture set standards for dress, lingo and behavioral codes — almost every aspect of how we comport ourselves in the world.

Cultural differences can breed misinterpretation; we're not always so effective at making accurate judgments outside our cultural comfort zone.

Different mental schemas can foster radically different behaviors. Failing to understand others' schemas — or being unaware of our own — can cause us to assign personality labels to people or stereotypes to groups, rather than working to understand the cultural values guiding the behavior.

◆ ◆ ◆

Now that we are aware of some of the basic problems that plague even the most highly trained diagnosticians, we are better equipped to spot our own biases. But our job is easier than theirs, because this book is not intended to be a clinical diagnostic tool, and making clinical assessments is not our objective.

Our goal is simply to learn to spot indicators of what is normal and healthy behavior and what is not. It is the job of the mental health professionals to label those indicators according to specific psychiatric disorders.

CHAPTER 3

The System at Work: Laying the Groundwork

I'm not crazy about reality,
but it's still the only place to get a decent meal.

GROUCHO MARX

We can assess a person without him ever being aware that he was being analyzed. The process doesn't require honesty, consent, or introspection from the person we are observing; every personality trait has a psychological signature that's almost impossible to hide. Our emotional selves manifest in behaviors that leave obvious and discernible traces, or *emotional footprints*. People simply can't help but give themselves away.

The Four-Facet Composite

We hear a lot about profiling in the media these days — racial profiling, psychological profiling, personal profiling, credit profiling, and so on. What is a profile? For our purposes, think of it as a representation of a person's prominent and distinctive characteristics — a snapshot.

To build an emotional profile, we begin by examining the four primary psychological (or hidden) facets from which a multitude of (observable) emotional footprints will emerge.

The Four Facets to emotional health are:

- Self-Esteem
- Responsibility
- Degree of Perspective
- Relationships and Boundaries

In Chapter 1, we presented an overview of the psychology of human nature, which will be useful in gaining a general understanding of our subject, especially when a person doesn't fit neatly into scoring templates.

The next four chapters explore each of the Four Facets in greater detail. When working in tandem, they create a synergistic chain to emotional health. For example, if we suffer from problems within the facet of *Responsibility* (Facet 2), if we can't control our behaviors, if we seek immediate gratification or focus much of our energy on keeping up an image, we become angry with ourselves, and the result is *low self-esteem* (Facet 1). To compensate for these feelings of guilt and inadequacy, the ego engages — we become *egocentric*. Egocentricity narrows our *Perspective* (Facet 3); our view is filled with more of the self and less of the rest of the world. This makes us increasingly more sensitive and unstable. Our *Boundaries* (Facet 4) become blurry and our *Relationships* (Facet 4) suffer.

Facets provide a broad structure for organizing a person's emotional framework, and can include a path of footprints that are observable across a spectrum of scenarios and situations.

For example, Facet 2, *the degree to which we take responsibility for our lives,* is a reflection of a person's emotional health. But how do we gauge responsibility? One footprint within *responsibility* is trustworthiness or reliability. Can we count on the person to keep his word and behave with integrity? Does he follow through and deliver what he promised, even if the circumstances become more difficult? These behaviors are completely observable — even quantifiable.

In the latter chapters we will learn how to further quantify our observations: The Five-Minute CAT Scan, which allows us to assess a person's overall emotional health from brief interactions, and ultimately, Conversational Archeology, to dig deeper and build a more complete psychological profile.

SECTION 2

The Four Facets

CHAPTER 4

Facet 1: The Self-Esteem Machine

Self-respect is the fruit of discipline;
the sense of dignity grows with the ability
to say no to oneself.
ABRAHAM J. HESCHEL

Self-esteem is not about turning the proverbial other cheek. Rather, self-esteem allows us to observe a situation with crystal clear clarity and respond with objectivity. It's only when our ego becomes engaged that we begin to take things personally. We connect the dots of someone else's behavior to a place of hurt. Regardless of what is said or done to us, the minute we move from compassion to anger or to any other negative emotion we are observing life through a myopic lens.

We all have an ego and self-esteem is not an all-or-nothing proposition; rather, it runs along a continuum that includes many shades of gray. Therefore, emotional stability or instability exists along a continuum of varying degrees, too, and is observed in gradations.

The Emergence of Personality (Disorders)

We all suffer from low self-esteem to one degree or another. When self-esteem begins to erode, three distinct personality types are produced:

- **Compliant:** Low self-esteem and a dented ego
- **Arrogant:** Low self-esteem and an inflated ego
- **Avoidant:** Low self-esteem and a corrupted ego

In each case, our perspective shrinks and unhealthy aspects of our personality are maximized, filtered by our own unique insecurities. A person who has high self-esteem cannot have a large ego. Remember, the ego and self-esteem are opposite ends of the seesaw; when one goes up, the other must go down.

The Compliant Personality

The Compliant is typically highly introverted. She's usually reserved at work, or on foreign soil — anywhere that's not her element. When she's in control of a situation, however, the Compliant — usually a wallflower — may bloom. In that brief window, she may even exhibit extroverted attributes because she feels safe, comfortable, and confident.

She is quick to apologize, even when something is not her fault. She does favors for others that she doesn't really want to do because she fears not being liked. She rarely stands up for herself, as she doesn't feel her needs are important enough to defend, and certainly no more important than the needs of others. She is the quintessential people-pleaser.

Of course, there is such a thing as altruism. But she may prefer to look after others because it takes her away from her own problems and her own life.

These two forms of giving leave opposite emotional imprints. The distinction is *intention* — it's the difference between being robbed versus giving a donation. In both cases, money is going from one's person's hands to another, but one experience is empowering, the other is enfeebling and destructive.

Giving out of fear or guilt does nothing to enhance our self-esteem; in fact, quite the opposite. Fear or guilt-driven giving diminishes our self-esteem. Why? Because we aren't really *giving*; the other person is *taking*. We are being taken advantage of, with our consent.

In more extreme circumstances she may devote not just her time but her entire life to other people. She feels that she is not able to accomplish anything great in her own life, so, in order to feel a sense of purpose, she resigns herself to serving the good of others. While this behavior may mirror that of a person who devotes her life sincerely for the greater good of humanity, the motivation is quite different.

The Arrogant Personality

The Arrogant Personality needs to be the center of attention — always. Arrogant people are usually loud, easily frustrated, and big complainers. The arrogant person usually doesn't mind offending or insulting someone when he thinks it will make him look better or smarter in the eyes of others. His grandiose sense of self-importance masks the pain that results from his secret feelings of low self-worth. Unlike his Compliant counterpart, he demands constant praise and adulation from others, and may become angry when attention is diverted elsewhere.

This person's needs are more pressing than anyone else's, and the Arrogant Personality expects everyone around him to accommodate him, regardless of what is going on their lives. He has a general lack of empathy for others because he cannot feel anyone else's pain.

The Arrogant Personality may perform single acts of grandiosity — giving in a large way — but there's little if no follow-through (if it requires a modicum of effort), and he will forever remind others of his generosity; all the while, he manifests a general, "What have you done for me lately?" attitude to the world.

He is often a fierce competitor whose self-worth hangs in the balance of every competition, no matter how minor. To compensate for feelings of inadequacy, he will become, to varying degrees, controlling, narcissistic, self-absorbed, pushy, and full of bravado (false bravery). He is offended if his opinions and ideas are not accepted as gospel. The Arrogant Personality also insists that people understand (and accept) his point of view, even if they are complete disinterested in his opinion. He views their resistance as evidence that *their* egos are intruding, causing them to stubbornly ignore his sound advice.

This person can often be seen hitting, banging, and forcing inanimate objects to do his will. Just as he tries to impose control on people, he treats objects with the same disrespect.

A person with high self-esteem respects others, and is sensitive to avoid offending, embarrassing, or annoying other people. The arrogant person, however, does not respect others because a person can only give what he has. If he does not have self-respect, then what does he have to give?

The Avoidant Personality

In addition to the aforementioned types, less common, though certainly evident, is the person who is detached and distances himself from people. Does our subject exhibit avoidance behavior beyond natural shyness? Does he live a solitary life?

This is a person with low self-esteem who is hyper-fearful that he will be judged, criticized, rejected, or humiliated. Extreme avoidance behavior can prevent a person from living the life he truly desires and can ultimately result in, or may be the consequence of, an anxiety disorder such as agoraphobia.

In her book, *Our Inner Conflicts*, Dr. Karen Horney describes this persona:

Among the most striking is a need for self-sufficiency . . . like any other neurotic trend the need for independence is compulsive and indiscriminate . . . he may bitterly resent illness, considering it a humiliation because it forces him to depend on others. He may insist on acquiring his knowledge of any subject first hand; rather than take what others have said or written.

This attitude would make for splendid inner indepen-dence if it were not carried to absurd lengths . . . Any questioning or criticism from outside, any awareness of his own failure to measure up to the image, any real insight into the forces operating within him can make him explode or crumble. He must restrict his life lest he be exposed to such dangers. He must avoid tasks that he is not certain to master. He may even develop an aversion to effort of any kind.

Probably the worst drawback is the ensuing alienation from the self . . . the person loses interest in life because it is not he who lives it; he cannot make decisions because he does not know what he really wants.

Any type of conformity or pressure, whether to time, schedule, or in some cases, social graces, are scorned. He is unconventional and beats to nobody's drum but his own.

A Natural Cycle

These mentalities are not usually fixed. A person with low self-esteem often vacillates between personas of inferiority (the compliant mentality) and superiority (producing arrogance or avoidance), depending on the dominant personality mode at any given time. When a person is feeling inferior, he directs the negativity inward, manifesting hurt and sadness, and when a person is feeling superior, he directs the negativity outward, resulting in anger or isolation.

All of us, from time to time, vacillate between the above mindsets. As the old saying goes, "A person should carry two pieces of paper in his pocket. One that says, 'I am nothing but dust,' and the other that says 'The world was created only for my sake.'" The secret, it notes, is knowing which piece of paper to pull out when. When we lack self-esteem, we react to a situation with the wrong mentality or piece of paper.

The Self-Esteem Counterfeits

Evaluating someone's level of self-esteem is not difficult, but it can be confounding if we don't know what merits attention and what can be dismissed. Following are five myths about self-esteem and the corresponding counterfeits that will reveal what is worth paying attention to.

Counterfeit 1: *Self-Esteem Versus Ego*

Do not fall into the trap of believing that a person with an inflated ego likes himself. If he has an inflated ego, he's not content, no matter how much he *appears* to like himself. This is a fundamental law of human nature — a psychological equation that always yields the same result.

Counterfeit 2: *Self-Esteem Versus Confidence*

Self-esteem is often confused with confidence, but the two are actually wholly different, and making the distinction will be critical to our assessments. Confidence is how effective we feel within a specific area or situation, while self-esteem is how much we like ourselves and how worthy we believe we are of receiving the good things that life has to offer.

It's quite possible that an emotionally healthy person may feel good about herself, yet not feel certain that she will succeed in certain situations. (A person's confidence in a particular situation is rooted in a variety of factors: previous performance, experiences, feedback, and comparisons to others' performance.) For instance, someone who has high self-esteem may be a poor chess player, but she still likes herself. She will exhibit signs of decreased confidence when playing chess with a superior player, yet her overall sense of self-worth remains unaffected.

A person's inflated sense of self does not derive from extremely high levels of self-love, but rather, self-loathing (Rosenthal, 2005). To the untrained eye, a person who desires to have a greater sense of self-worth, and attempts to achieve it by emphasizing a specific trait or attribute (e.g. being the best tennis player at his athletic club), may *appear* to have high self-esteem. But it's not that simple, and usually an erroneous perception. A person's feelings of self-worth are more significantly impacted by her free will choices than by the assets at her disposal. So what may appear to be evidence of high self-esteem is in actual fact an inflated sense of confidence that is confined to a specific arena.

Counterfeit 3: *The Success Story*

We cannot gauge a person's self-esteem by how successful he appears to be. For instance, a partner in a major law firm may seem, to the casual observer, to be successful. But if his lifelong dream was to be a musician, and he abandoned his dream to appease someone else, or to gain the attention or respect of others, he cannot generally enjoy high self-esteem because his decision was motivated by fear.

Conversely, an artist who doesn't have much money may not be the traditional societal notion of success, but if he is achieving his dream and fulfilling his genuine desire, he'll have the opportunity to experience higher self-esteem. If our decisions hinge on outside approval or acceptance, we will always be looking to the rest of the world for emotional reinforcement.

Counterfeit 4: *Humility or Weakness?*

It's easy to mistake humility for weakness. But in actual fact, the opposite is true. Humility signifies strength and a high level of self-esteem (Ryan, 1983). People who demonstrate humility usually have more self-control and live more fulfilled lives.

An arrogant person, on the other hand, takes. He's an emotional junkie — enslaved to impulses he cannot rise above, forever dependent on others to feed his fragile ego.

As we will learn in later chapters, when assessing the trait of humility, we have to take care to filter out false positives. Is the person under observation acquiescing to the wishes of others, not because he wants to do the right thing, but because he's afraid to say "No," or does not feel worthy of asserting himself? We have to distinguish between those who are humble and enjoy high self-esteem and those who allow themselves to become doormats, where the person is merely *acting* humble to get other people to like him, or to assuage feelings of guilt or inadequacy.

Counterfeit 5: *Self-Esteem Versus Mood*

Generally speaking, people with high self-esteem tend to have a pleasant and positive demeanor; but we can't necessarily gauge a person's self-esteem by his disposition in a single instance — mood can get in the way. A person may appear to be in a good mood — outgoing, warm, and engaging — while, in actuality, he is a self-absorbed narcissist who is simply able to adopt a false persona for a short period of time.

Self-esteem is an internal setting that keeps running throughout our daily lives. Like the temperature setting on our air-conditioner, our self-esteem set-point remains fairly consistent, whether it is set at a chilly 62 degrees, a mild 74 degrees, or a sizzling 80 degrees.

Mood is transient and fleeting — it can change from minute to minute, hour to hour, day to day. It can also shift in response to external factors, such as hearing some good (or bad) news, or to internal factors, such as hunger (or overeating).

A person with high self-esteem can certainly be in a bad mood if he gets yelled at by his boss, has a flat tire, or waits too long to eat lunch before that afternoon conference call. But his self-esteem is not negatively affected by those circumstances, and the unpleasant state will soon fade. In our chapter on perspective, we will see how, for people with high self-esteem, bad moods are less frequent and don't last as long as they might for someone with lower self-esteem.

To conclude, we can't assume that someone has low self-esteem just because he's in a bad mood. Nor can we assume that he has high self-esteem just because he's smiling or running to help an elderly lady cross the street.

So How Can We Tell?

A person who lacks self-esteem may overindulge his desires, while not treating others particularly well (a product of the arrogant or avoidant mentality). Or this person may devote so much time and energy to gaining the approval and respect of others that he fails to take care of his own needs (a product of the compliant mentality). A person with high self-esteem, on the other hand, strikes a balance—he is able to give love, respect, time, and attention to both himself and to others.

One particularly revealing insight into a person's psyche is evaluating how he treats those he "doesn't have to be nice to" and doesn't need to impress, such as the waiter, receptionist, or doorman compared to how he interacts with those who can do something for him or his career. Does he generally strive to be respectful to others? Or is he only respectful to those from whom he wants something?

Be on alert for the two-faced person whose personality is inconsistent. He might be nice to us, but not so polite to others. (Of course, if he treats us poorly but others well, we already know we've got a problem.) The former is a concern because it indicates that he's adjusting his conduct toward us for his own gain; his behavior toward us is not a reflection of his true nature.

Yes, It Begins in Childhood

One can gain insight into a person's emotional health by taking a look at his childhood relationships (as well as his adult relationships). When a child is not nurtured and loved, or is raised in a turbulent, traumatic family dynamic that leaves him constantly feeling that his life is out of control, his self-esteem is negatively impacted, and may remain damaged as an adult.

Children gain self-esteem largely from their parents (or primary caregivers). Children do not possess the reasoning faculties to make choices like adults do, thus they cannot gain self-respect through self-control. A more objective sense of right and wrong is not fully established until our early teens.

Children, who are egocentric beings, often blame themselves for their parents' behavior. When a parent becomes angry with the child, the child naturally concludes that she must be flawed. She translates her parent's anger to *I am unworthy of his love*, which soon becomes *I am not worthy of being loved*.

Now, if a child can form these conclusions (as many do) when they are raised by loving parents, imagine how easy it is for the child, who is being raised by abusive parents, to conclude that she's unlovable or flawed. Most likely, she will think to herself: *If my own parents can do this to me, what can I possibly be worth?*

If children don't receive love from their parents, or grow up in volatile homes, they may literally spend the rest of their lives craving love and acceptance. All their efforts, in one way or another, are dedicated to finding love and acceptance; this brings us to the subject of divorce.

Linda Waite and Maggie Gallagher cited these statistics

in the book, *The Case for Marriage: Why Married People are Healthier, Happier, and Better-Off Financially:*

> Divorce doubles the risk that children will experience serious psychological problems later in life, even after controlling for pre-divorce characteristics. A large Swedish study found that as adults, children raised in single-parent families were 56 percent more likely to show signs of mental illness than children from intact married homes. Two recent studies followed identical and non-identical twins in Australia who married and had children, enabling the researchers to control for genetic factors that might play a role in mental health outcomes . . . The researchers found that the children of divorce in this sample were significantly more likely to suffer from mental illness, addictions, and thoughts of suicide . . . A study of 534 Iowa families found that divorce increased the risk of depression in children.

Although many children adapt perfectly well to divorce or separation, the statistics suggest that marital rifts can ultimately contribute to significant red flag behaviors. Children are aware when their parents are fighting or are unhappy. How parents handle everyday marital conflicts significantly impacts a child's emotional security, and ultimately his ability to build positive relationships with others. Studies show that destructive marital conflict (personal insults, defensiveness, marital withdrawal, sadness or fear) set in motion events that lead to later emotional insecurity and maladjustment in children, which can manifest as depression, anxiety, and behavioral problems (Cummings, 2006).

But there's a flipside. When couples deal with marital conflict by demonstrating physical affection, engaging in problem solving, and agreeing to compromise, a child's emotional security is increased as a result of witnessing such positive interaction between his parents, and such behavior serves as a model for effective conflict resolution.

Of course, it must be considered that a child may ultimately be happier being a product of divorced parents, when the alternative is being raised in an unstable and turbulent environment.

◆ ◆ ◆

We may have been influenced and impacted by our past and the people in it — our parents, teachers, friends — but what we do today is up to us. Our life is now in our own hands. Sink or swim. Every action we take today influences what kind of person we will become tomorrow. No greater freedom exists than being responsible for our own future.

If we spend our adult years blaming others, rather than

taking responsibility for our actions, our self-esteem suffers. Conversely, if we choose to accept responsibility for our lives, regardless of our troubled past, we begin to infuse ourselves with a greater sense of self-worth.

Next, we will see precisely how responsibility links with self-esteem to reveal a more complete emotional picture.

CHAPTER 5

Facet 2: The Responsibility Factor

I can resist everything except temptation.

OSCAR WILDE

T he quality of our emotional lives is directly proportional to the amount of responsibility we are willing to accept. Renowned psychiatrist, Dr. William Glasser, in his timeless classic, *Reality Therapy*, writes: "People do not act irresponsibly because they are ill; they are ill because they act irresponsibly." If we continue to blame our unhappiness on external factors, we will never move forward.

In order to grow emotionally, in order to progress in life, there needs to be change. Giving up the familiar can prove to be challenging. We are afraid to lose what we have, and, more painfully, the comfort and security that goes with it.

If we tell ourselves that we are going to fail, then we can resign ourselves to our current situation, and need not feel guilty for opting out. By adopting such attitudes as, "I am thirty-five years old — there's no chance I will get married" or "All the good ideas have already been thought of," we can avoid even trying.

With poor emotional health we are unwilling to invest any more of ourselves unless we can be assured of a payoff. At the start of a task there's little risk, but as we expend more energy, we become concerned that this is going to be "another one of those times," and we quickly look for an out. The cycle continues as we jump from idea to idea. Our energy comes only in bursts and is never sustained.

We also become increasingly discouraged because we are not able to focus on the outcome. In our mind, obstacles are not barriers to be overcome but are hazards to be avoided and warning signs to quit. We will put in effort where there's a guarantee of success or at least a high certainty that we will succeed. The reward — no matter what it is — must be immediate in order to provide any satisfaction whatsoever. This attitude breeds extreme personalities who become addicted to instant gratification, leapfrogging from task to task, relationship to relationship each time an emotional payoff comes due. We may even manufacture gratification opportunities in order to feel the thrill of life without actually having to live. Does the following scenario remind you of anyone you know?

> I'm ready to leave my house, but now I have to play the usual game of hide-and-seek with my keys. I finally find them after a brief search. When I return home, will I put them where I'll be able to find them? Of course not. And keys aren't the only thing I lose. Sometimes I even lose my car! I don't always take notice of where I parked my car, even though I know that means I'll have to endure the usual ten-minute search. The file that I absolutely cannot lose is the object of another search-and-find mission. My wallet, purse, phone book, coupons, registration — just about everything and anything that I can misplace, I will.

Certainly, it's possible to be occasionally careless or absent-minded. Sometimes we're preoccupied, have a lot on our minds — it happens to the best of us. But if we continually lose or misplace items of value, there's probably another explanation.

By misplacing items, we create mini-obstacles for ourselves that must be overcome. Once the misplaced item is found, we derive a sense of satisfaction. We create an artificial challenge in a controlled environment that, once overcome, gives us a sense of accomplishment, which puts us in a better mood. The thrill of this challenge, though, is never consciously examined. To illustrate:

Let's say we're driving along; we're in a fair mood — not in a great mood, but not in a bad mood, either. We then notice flashing lights in the rearview mirror . . . we're being pulled over for speeding. The usual routine ensues — "License, registration, insurance, please." Then, much to our surprise, we're let off with a warning. As we pull back onto the highway, now find ourselves in a buoyant mood. "What good fortune!" we think to ourselves.

But why? What just happened? What in our life has changed? Absolutely nothing! The reason why we're in such a good mood is because we have emerged from the situation as victors. That's the payoff.

Think about it. When setting up these little challenges for ourselves, we would never "lose" our heart medication. Nor would we toss our keys into the ocean and expect to find them later. The goal is to feel a sense of accomplishment, which can only happen if we find whatever is missing without drastically disrupting our lives.

This reward-seeking response may manifest itself in small, everyday behaviors; for example, refusing to move the serving bowl closer to our plate when serving ourselves, or not centering our mug directly under the coffeepot spout while pouring — preferring to pour at a distance. We are manufacturing small challenges in order to feel a sense of accomplishment. Where is the satisfaction in serving oneself if there's no chance it could spill all over the table?

In some instances, we may actually create these little challenges because, unconsciously, we want to inconvenience ourselves. Feelings of guilt and self-recrimination cause us to inflict harm upon ourselves. (Note that this is the very epitome of self-destruction.)

Emotional independence is not about being able to indulge whatever we feel like doing whenever we feel like doing it; rather, it's about being able to do what we truly *want* to do, in spite of what we feel like doing at the moment. There's a difference between *wanting* to do something and *feeling* like doing something. Wanting taps into intellect, our souls — responsible, conscious choice. Feeling is an emotionally-based desire that may sometimes run counter to what we wish we could do, if only we could rise above our impulses.

Imagine being on a diet and suddenly feeling the urge to eat a piece of chocolate. We fight the temptation for a while, but eventually give in. Is that freedom or slavery? We felt like eating a piece of chocolate, so we did. Did we like how we felt afterward? Probably not. When we rise above our temptations and resist them, we exercise self-control. And that's when we experience true freedom and emotional health.

Freedom is the crux of self-respect. It is difficult to feel good about ourselves when we are unnaturally dependent on someone or something. It's an uncomfortable, perhaps debilitating, feeling.

In order to feel good, we must *do* good; it's only when we're able to choose responsibly that we gain self-respect and, in turn, self-esteem. *Doing* the right thing is the mechanism that intertwines self-respect and self-control. We only gain self-esteem — the core of psychological health — when we're able to make responsible choices, and choose to do what's right, regardless of what we feel like doing or how our choice will appear to others.

Responsibility manifests itself in three distinct attributes: acceptance, delaying gratification, and morality.

Accepting Responsibility Means Accepting Reality

When reality clashes with our willingness to accept it, the ensuing disconnect creates an internal conflict called *cognitive dissonance*. Under this burdensome psychological weight, those who suffer from poor emotional health constantly feel the need to justify themselves and their actions to themselves and to the world. They have to make sense of their choices in the least painful way possible. The result? *Being right* becomes more of an emotional priority than *doing what is right*.

Our instincts protect our psychological wellbeing in much the same way that we consciously protect our physical bodies. When our physical welfare is threatened, a natural fight-or-flight response is engaged. Similarly, when our psychological wellbeing is threatened, we engage our accept-or-deflect response. When a mind is healthy and strong, a challenge to the self is usually accepted and confronted directly. But a mind that is not healthy may try to deflect the threat.

Just as a physically weak person will shy away from physical challenges, deflection becomes a conditioned response for the psychologically weak. A person who is emotionally unwell instinctively reacts to conflicts in the following ways: "You're wrong" or "This is just how I am." There is also little room for "I was wrong" or any acknowledgment of personal responsibility.

This person deflects the world and his own insecurities, and, in the process, loses self-esteem because the psychological self can only develop through acceptance. The accept-or-deflect response is our emotional immune system. In the person who lacks self-esteem, the deflection response is engaged at all times. Everything is perceived as a threat to his psychological wellbeing. Nothing is ever accepted, so no growth can ever occur.

Every time we refuse to acknowledge the truth about any aspect of ourselves (or condemn ourselves for being imperfect), we send the unconscious message, "I am inadequate." As an analogy, today's vehicles are designed so that, in an accident, the vehicle absorbs as much of the collision's kinetic energy as possible. This absorbed energy cannot be recovered, since it goes into the permanent deformation of the vehicle — the resulting dents. When we collide with reality and refuse to accept it, we become emotionally dented.

There's nothing wrong with seeing ourselves as less than perfect. It's honest and healthy. But that healthy acceptance of imperfection is a far cry from obsessing over our imperfections and condemning ourselves as worthless or lacking. Self-condemnation can only lower our self-esteem.

Delaying Gratification: Why Smart People Make Dumb Choices

In any given situation, it's quite possible for a smart person to make an astonishingly poor decision, while his less-intelligent counterpart will make the wiser, more prudent, choice.

It is our self-esteem, not our intellect, which actually steers us toward a choice. Self-esteem and emotional wellbeing go hand-in hand. Intelligence, however, is largely unrelated to either self-esteem or emotional wellbeing.

Let's look at this another way: An overweight diabetic

with low self-esteem knows she shouldn't be eating chocolate cake for dinner, but she eats it anyway. Her low self-esteem is directing the choice she makes. In that moment, she's more interested in the chocolate cake than in her physical health.

In my book, "You Can Read Anyone," (Lieberman, 2007) the motivation is explained as follows: Self-esteem dictates what we're interested in and what we become attracted to. When our self-esteem is low, our interest (and vision) shifts from long-term to immediate — if it feels good, do it, regardless of the consequences. The most appealing choice will be the one that satisfies our immediate needs and wants — be it for ego-oriented or body-oriented desires.

We're like the child who would rather have one lollipop now than five lollipops tomorrow. Five lollipops, of course, is the better bargain, but the child is not thinking about that. His focus is short-term, shallow, and narrow. Immediate gratification is all that matters.

Someone who has low self-esteem is as emotionally immature as the child who chooses the single lollipop; he's primarily interested in the here and now. This shortsightedness causes him to forsake the choice that would be in his best interest in the long run, and by extension, choices that would be in the best interest of others. He isn't motivated to benefit others unless the choice will satisfy his own ulterior, selfish motives.

When self-esteem increases, however, a person becomes

much more interested in, and attracted to, alternatives that offer long-term satisfaction. He finds pleasure in more meaningful objectives — pursuits that will benefit him in the long-term, even at the cost of immediate gratification.

Yes, the smartest people can do the stupidest — most illogical — things. Even though they may possess the mental fuel (i.e., intellect), they lack the clarity (perspective) to steer the wheel in the right direction. Intelligence can only put us in the driver's seat with a map in hand. Wisdom, which is one of the most powerful byproducts of emotional stability, gives us the capacity and fortitude to steer the car in the right direction.

There is no status quo in nature. The Law of Conservation states that organisms die if they don't grow. Human beings are wired to feel pleasure when they're productive. Pleasure is attached to *meaning*. When we do what's right — and seek meaning over temporary gratification — we gain pleasure; when we don't, we may feel anxious or depressed.

Depression is aptly described then as a taste of death. This is because our soul yearns to grow, so when a person is not moving his life in the direction of proper growth, this feeling of futility—going around in circles—feels to the soul like death.

Lying on the couch watching TV is comfortable, but not meaningful, and so, by definition, offers little, if any, lasting pleasure. To be more precise, the feeling we experience as a couch potato is not really pleasure at all but comfort, which is the avoidance of pain. If we seek to avoid pain, we must avoid life.

Low self-esteem or poor emotional health is the force behind the impulse that urges us to satiate the appetites of the ego and body. When we don't achieve true pleasure (meaningful pleasure), we grab whatever thrills we can find wherever we can find them. We may even deceive ourselves into believing that what we're doing is important because that makes us feel relevant.

We'll even attach meaning to nonsense, attempting to convince ourselves and others that what we're doing has significance, when we know, deep down, that we're only seeking to justify wasting time on meaningless activities.

The more engaged we are, the more meaningful our life is, and the more pleasurable our experiences. The more one withdraws into temporary comforts, or pursues illusions driven by the ego, the less pleasurable life becomes. We may sometimes feel productive, but deep down, we realize that our pursuits are not fulfilling. No matter how much effort we expend, the satisfaction will be fleeting because the end achievement is not meaningful. Being comfortable and having fun are not enough; our soul gnaws at us, not just to *do* more, but to *become* something more.

In assessing the behavior of others, it's valuable to know whether a person is willing to endure the arrows and slings . . .

HAMLET: ACT 3, SCENE 1

To be or not to be, that is the question.
Whether to withstand the slings and arrows
of outrageous fortune,
or by taking arms against a sea of troubles . . .
Or to take arms against a sea of troubles,
And by opposing, end them? To die: to sleep;
No more; and by a sleep to say we end
The heart-ache and the thousand natural shocks . . .

Shakespeare speaks of the struggle we are confronted with each day when literally making hundreds of decisions. Will we face life head-on, endure the struggle, and seek to triumph, or will we turn away from what is right and seek the comfort of illusionary pleasures? There is also a third dark and sad choice: We can choose to end our lives in order to escape the torment. But those are the choices.

People who demand immediate gratification—"I want it all and I want it now!"—are emotionally insecure. To fill the emptiness created by an unhealthy self-image, they surrender to the body's need to feel good and the ego's need to look good by demanding immediate and instant gratification.

Those who spend recklessly or live beyond their means attempt to bolster their feelings of low self-worth with material belongings. The accumulation of possessions· is a futile effort to fill the emptiness inside. Additionally, "keeping up with the Jones's" is the ego's way of projecting an image of worth and value to others. Naturally, the void constantly needs to be replenished and the image typically requires more and more things to be sustained.

Financial responsibility is absolutely not about how much wealth a person accumulates. Rather, based on a person's means, does he spend money responsibly or irresponsibly? A person who lives within his means has the discipline to set boundaries and control any reckless impulses he may have. Impulses are, after all, normal; acting on them, however, is not always healthy.

Moral Compass

Narrow values and limited perspective are built on low self-esteem. When we are unable to rise above our own wants and needs, we align our values with our own desires. Instead of raising our consciousness, we lower the bar.

Tolerance and acceptance of others shows a broad healthy value base, which usually translates across other life scenarios. People who are emotionally unwell, however, will adopt beliefs and values that are morally corrupt in order to accommodate their insecurities. Any form of prejudice is a vain attempt to explain why one is disadvantaged, without accepting personal responsibility.

We all, to varying degrees, know the difference between right and wrong. Though it has no specific locus in the physical body, morality is hard-wired into the human species through a mechanism we call conscience.

With rare exceptions, we all know, for example, that murder is wrong. Even if we're brought up in a morally questionable environment, there's an internal discomfort that tells us something isn't quite right. No matter how masterfully they can justify it, even those who do murder know it's wrong — at some point they realize that they wouldn't appreciate someone hurting them or their loved ones. Then how are they able to keep killing, perhaps repeatedly? The whisper of conscience eventually gets drowned out by the repeated rationalizations they make to themselves.

What is the substance of the moral compass? One's integrity, honesty, and authenticity—and whether they manifest themselves in a healthy or self-serving way. White lies, for example, are the lubricant of a civil society, and are not a reliable indication of poor emotional health whatsoever. People may understandably lie to protect privacy, to avoid being embarrassed, or to avoid danger to themselves or others. Unreserved honesty is not always the best policy.

However, if a person misrepresents himself, tries to convince others that he's someone he's not, or that he has accomplished something he hasn't, it's a sign of manipulation; and that he may be a person who will sacrifice integrity to get approval, build affinity, or gain trust.

◆ ◆ ◆

When we behave irresponsibly, the need to maintain a false image of ourselves grows. The ego engages to compensate for our feelings of guilt and self-contempt, and narrows our perspective of the world. In the next chapter, we will examine in greater depth how a limited perspective makes people increasingly sensitive and unstable.

CHAPTER 6

Facet 3: Degree of Perspective

The pessimist sees difficulty in every opportunity.
The optimist sees the opportunity in every difficulty.
WINSTON CHURCHILL

The psychological mechanics of perspective are intriguing. Here's how it works:

A person sustains severe injuries in an accident and works tirelessly to regain the use of his legs. He will likely experience immense and lasting gratitude when his ability to walk is restored. On the other hand, the gratitude of someone who narrowly avoids an accident dissipates in just moments. How can these two very different reactions be explained? Surely the more fortunate one, who avoided injury altogether, should be more grateful than the one who sustained serious injuries. After all, the one who emerged unscathed didn't have to endure painful surgeries or months of rehabilitation.

Even more amazing, a person who didn't even have to swerve to avoid the accident (and possibly incur a lapful of scalding coffee) typically feels little, if any, gratitude.

Isn't it odd that a person who survives and triumphs over disaster is filled with lasting gratitude; a person who dodges the accident feels fleeting gratitude (which perhaps even ultimately shifts to annoyance); and when nothing happens at all, we simply grumble about the traffic? What's the explanation?

The reason that gratitude is so often fleeting is that we believe what we have or what we get is deserved — we have a sense of *entitlement*. If we found ourselves traveling through a war zone and managed to reach our destination safely, we'd likely be grateful. But, if we don't perceive traveling as a physical threat, then getting from point A to point B unharmed holds little meaning for us. Why should we feel grateful for something we've come to expect? This is how it's supposed to be, after all. We are entitled.

It's only when reality conflicts with expectations that we realize our inalienable rights can suddenly be denied. The person who drives uneventfully experiences no threat to his wellbeing. From his perspective, life is as it should be. But, after a near miss, he recognizes that the *possibility* of unfulfilled expectations (or disaster) exists, so he feels *some* gratitude that his entitlements were not stripped from him. This effect is magnified after a serious accident occurs because his world, his reality, has changed forever. His ability to walk again is not guaranteed, so when he *does* regain the use of his legs, he views it as a gift.

The wider and deeper our perspective in life, the more permanent and deep our gratitude. Nothing needs to happen to make us feel good. We simply appreciate what we have.

When we are egocentric, we become angry and frustrated with life for disappointing us. Our expectations are never met, and we're consumed with thoughts of what we lack, and what is owed to us. Happiness eludes us. We're always one step away from feeling complete and we'll search endlessly for that next great thing that promises to bring us lasting fulfillment.

It says in the Bible, "Who is wealthy? He who is happy with his lot." This one phrase provides a wealth of insight into human nature. The flipside is that one who is not happy with what he has will become envious, jealous, crave honor and respect — all functions of the ego and sure indicators of low self-esteem.

General Attitude, Overall Disposition, and Mood Fluctuation

The attributes of an unhealthy person can usually be characterized as behaviors that exemplify a child-like manner. We should always ask ourselves if the person is responding to a situation like a child would — sudden tantrums, mindless exuberance, wild mood swings, an absolute, black-white-view of events.

Is the person's mood inconsistent or erratic — up one minute and down the next? Is his mood like a leaf drifting on the whims of the wind — constantly, shifting from fortune to crisis? How much and often does his mood fluctuate? Huge spikes or dips in a person's emotional energy level can be a reliable indicator; in the extreme, such moods may be indicative of Bipolar Disorder (or Borderline Personality Disorder).

Becoming exuberant over trivial things is as unhealthy as getting upset over ridiculous things. For instance, if someone's mood suddenly soars because he got a green light even though he's not in a rush and has nowhere to go, pay attention.

When a person overreacts to every situation — from a headache to a stubbed toe — it is a clear sign that his perspective is off. Missed parking spaces, sold-out movies, and lost lotteries are all part of life's minor disappointments. They don't bother the emotionally stable person. He doesn't dwell on them because he recognizes them for what they are — small, insignificant events.

When trying to assess a person's emotional state, another question needs to be asked. What does this person tend to complain about? Nonsense, such as scratches on his dining room floor? Or are the grievances, really questions, and more meaningful, indicating an attempt on his part to understand his world and the difficulties that he faces?

Renowned psychologist and creator of Rational Emotive Behavior Therapy (REBT), Albert Ellis, has proposed three core beliefs or philosophies that function as the window through which people tend to perceive themselves. These core beliefs are each filtered through our language, and identifying these beliefs can give us a better picture of a person's inner world.

According to Ellis, we can look at any given situation and determine whether people are inclined toward a certain predisposition of irrational thinking.

REBT says that at the core of irrational beliefs, there are rigid demands and commands, and that certain language cues, such as the tendency to awfulize, frustration, intolerance, deprecation of others, and over-generalizations, are accompanied by these irrational beliefs.

For instance, in an unconscious attempt to anchor ourselves in something definitive, a person may paint his world in black and white. This is unless, of course, the perspective does not suit him, in which case he may suddenly begin to see shades of gray when the truth is in fact objective and clear.

Being able to discern nuances in our life is part of a wider, healthier perspective. Probe whether or not the person only engages in selective memory, like a child who says, "You never let me . . . " as opposed to the healthier and more balanced variation: "Sometimes you don't let me . . . " Another common example might include: "If I don't get this, I'll never be happy . . . "

The use of harsh language, just like speaking in absolutes, is a clear indicator that something is not quite right at the core. Rather than making a simple, accurate claim like 'This clock isn't working anymore," someone says, "The clock is busted to pieces!" It is an almost childlike perspective that evokes an image of a tantrum, during which the clock has been thrown around the room and destroyed.

Abrasive language suggests that the person may not always view situations from an appropriate perspective. They associate previous experiences with violence or destruction, which either excited or enthralled them, and they seek to relive those experiences in relatively benign settings.

Consider statements like: "I really blistered my knee to ribbons" or "My performance has completely devastated the team." These statements exhibit both absolute (black-or-white) tendencies, as well as violent, harsh, or overstated language. Statements like, "We had a huge blowup over the schedule," and "I ripped him to pieces in the interview" also use harsh words with violent undertones which may seem insignificant at first glance, but may suggest something more troubling under the surface.

Dodging Those Blind Spots

It is perspective that determines how we perceive the world and respond to it. The clearer and sharper our perspective, the more reality we let in, and the more objective and rational our attitudes, thoughts, and behaviors.

Attempting to navigate the world through the limited perspective of low self-esteem is like trying to navigate a ship through fog and cloud so dense that we can barely see our hand in front of our face.

When our horizon is a limited perspective, perceptions of all the people and objects around us are easily distorted, even when the decision before us has an objectively obvious right choice. In other words, the lower our self-esteem, the cloudier our decision-making ability. When we lose our sanity, we have lost all perspective. Sanity is simply perspective — the ability to see reality clearly.

You've probably had the experience of trying to explain something to someone who is quite bright, but is simply not getting it. We figure that if we just present a rational argument and explain the facts clearly and logically, he'll cruise to the right conclusion and see things our way (which, of course, happens to be the right way).

Odds are, however, that he's not thinking *logically*, so attempting to *reason* with him is futile. His response is based on his feelings; thus, his conclusions are emotionally charged, rather than based on reason. His perspective of the situation is too narrow, and instead of seeing an accurate view of reality, he sees a projection of his own wants and needs.

In fact, this is precisely the type of person who prides himself on his instincts — because he routinely disregards logic (though he paradoxically sees himself as a man of intellect). He's the person who says, "You have to go with your gut" and "trust your intuition, no matter what." He's thinking emotionally, rather than rationally; thus, the facts often conflict with how his ego needs to view the world.

"How can he be so foolish?" we wonder. We're still looking for the logic behind a rationale that doesn't exist. We're looking for reason in a psychological landscape devoid of reason.

But here's the irony: Who's more rational? The person who cannot hear the truth when it's spoken to him, or the person who desperately continues trying to speak truth to someone who isn't listening? If we become angry, frustrated, or annoyed because someone else is simply not getting it, we're behaving even more irrationally than he is. The other person cannot help himself. But we know better, and can choose to end this exercise in futility.

We all have our blind spots, little dark pockets of bias and illogic into which the light of reality simply does not shine. When someone is behaving in a way that we perceive to be irrational, we may be stunned by the absurdity of the situation

— we may even see him as *crazy*. But what we may not be seeing is that his blind spots are simply different than ours.

Decision-Making

In order to be an effective decision-maker, it is crucial to strike the balance and avoid both procrastination and impulsivity. Procrastination is one of the ego's favorite tool, and is deceptively clever in the way it works.

The tasks we have to accomplish on a day-to-day basis may be very minor — all we have to do is stamp the envelope and mail the letter, move a box that has been in our way for two months, check our voice mail, or send a thank-you note to our relatives — but we don't. We constantly put off the most simple of tasks.

We fail to complete minor and non-threatening tasks so that our attention is occupied all the time. In this way, we can avoid having to think about, and deal with, larger issues in our lives that really do require urgent attention.

The impact of this behavior is compounded. The conscious rationale we feed ourselves with is, "I've got more important things to worry about. I can't fuss with these little things." In this way, our lives spiral beyond control, and nothing ends up getting done. The small things are never dealt with so that we can avoid thinking about the bigger things, and the big things remain undone because our thoughts are occupied with the little things. Ultimately we become overwhelmed, so we waste our time on passive acts, such as watching TV.

Very often we use our everyday tasks as an excuse to opt out of life. Letting the minor things pile up gives us the illusion that our lives are complicated, productive, busy, and maybe even fulfilled. Our perspective, which is narrowed, relieves us of the burden of looking at the larger picture.

As well as the importance of avoiding procrastination in the decision-making process, we also have to make sure that we do not allow ourselves to be impulsive. Impulsivity in responsible doses can be likened to spontaneity, enthusiasm, and passion for life. But sometimes a lack of self-control can lead to impulsive decisions, where the ramifications are not fully — if at all — considered before a decision is made.

The ideal balance is acting with consideration, where we weigh the consequences carefully and realistically before we move forward.

Flexibility: Abandon Ship or Fight to the Death?

The second component to effective decision-making lies in the capacity to let go of what is no longer productive in our lives. We are taught from childhood to persevere, to finish what we start. But as hard as it may be to admit defeat and throw in the towel, investing all of our time and energy into a pursuit or venture that is going nowhere is certainly not productive.

Clearly, a balanced perspective is about more than perseverance and steadfast commitment. It's also about knowing when to cut our losses and channel our energy into more productive options.

Poor emotional health forces us to defend our choices and justify our actions more aggressively. We often find it difficult to reject false or damaging beliefs and behaviors, even when we know they're hurting us. High self-esteem gives us the emotional fuel to release outdated or warped ideas or behaviors.

Loss aversion refers to our ego's tendency to lean towards avoiding loss over acquiring gains. It's not just that we can't stand losing; we can't stand even the *possibility* of losing.

We slip into loss aversion gear so easily . . .

Jack, a day trader, gets a hot tip on a new "can't-miss" stock. He has such great expectations that he violates his own rule of never risking more than 5 percent of his stake on any one stock. At 8 am, he buys 250 shares at $28 per share — $7000, 10 percent of his total stake.

But the stock starts tanking . . . he begins to sweat . . .

By noon, it's down to $23 . . . he's lost $1250, but that's okay, it'll go back up — he's certain of it! By 1 pm, it's down to $21 . . . he's lost $1750, but he'll ride it down, he won't sell, oh no — in fact, *this is the time to double down!* He buys another 250 shares for $5250. When the stock goes back up, he'll cover his loss. It'll work, it *must* work —

But it doesn't. Two minutes before closing bell, he finally cashes in . . . at $16 per share. He's lost $6750. And all because he couldn't bear to cut his losses and move on to the next trade. He was so desperate to make up for his loss that he was oblivious to the risks of staying in the game.

Poor Jack continued to ride the stock down, even though the odds were stacked against him. Why do rational people sometimes make irrational decisions? Why are we willing to throw away good money after bad? As any master stock trader will tell you, we start losing money the second we allow our emotions to influence our trading decisions. When investors put on blinders, ignore empirical evidence, and dedicate themselves to recovering as much of their loss as possible, we say they're chasing a loss.

And this is the first law of loss aversion: When we start playing to *not lose*, rather than playing to win, we are chasing a loss. When we focus on avoiding losses, rather than focusing on maximizing our gains, we have already lost. (This is not to suggest that a person who is an effective day-trader is emotionally healthier than those who may lose money. The former is able to compartmentalize his behavior, and in specific situations, contain his emotions.)

According to the economic view of behavior, people are aware, rational, and in control of major financial decisions. Behavioral psychology, however, suggests something else entirely: We are often completely unaware of the unconscious forces that drive our decisions.

We make choices by assigning values to different options, then we commit. Our commitment to staying the course tends to become stronger once we have invested time, money, or energy into something — whether it's a tumbling stock, a doomed relationship, or a dead-end job. If we make a hopeless investment, it's easy to succumb to the sunk-cost fallacy: *I can't stop now because everything I've invested so far will be lost!* This is true, of course, but it's irrelevant to whether we should continue to invest. Everything we have already invested is lost. Nothing can be done to change that. Misguided commitment may even become a delay tactic: We (the ego) can't bear to face the consequences of our poor judgment.

The ego, which is the glue that bonds our self-concept to our values and behaviors, can be quite resistant to changing course. When someone has invested themselves into someone or something, the ego makes it harder for him to walk away, even from a situation that has become intolerable. If that person's perspective is warped, so is his thinking, and this may manifest in the typical *co-dependent* behavior that therapists have become so adept at identifying in recent decades.

Now we know why car salesmen keep us waiting for so long after they leave the room to "talk to the manager" about that deal we proposed. They know that the more time we spend there, the more invested we'll become, and the harder it will be to just get up and leave.

◆ ◆ ◆

Footprints that betray a narrow perspective and lack of gratitude reveal insights into a person's emotional health. Those footprints, as we will discover in the next chapter, can track mud through our relationships and our lives.

CHAPTER 7

Facet 4: Relationships and Boundaries

> *No man is an island entire of itself;*
> *every man is a piece of the continent,*
> *a part of the main.*
>
> JOHN DONNE

Our lives are not simply colored by our relationships, they are defined by them. The ability to form and maintain good relationships is central to our health and happiness (Crossley & Langdrige, 2005). While we might all occasionally yearn to be an island unto ourselves, we know it's virtually impossible to *not* have to rely on, and interact with, others.

Even when we do get a rare break from humanity, by escaping to a tropical island getaway or self-imposed solitary confinement, it is inevitable that we will start craving human contact. We begin to miss the stimulation of good conversation, the joy of others' laughter, and simply the comforting sound of other humans speaking.

Not only are our lives defined by relationships, we, as humans, are defined by our intrinsic and relentless need to create them. We begin this lifelong relationship odyssey with our parents, siblings, and friends. From the time we're infants, we are (if we're fortunate) practically bombarded by the intimacy, familiarity, and warmth of human relationships. Early on, we find ourselves thrust into social settings, such as the neighbor's sandbox, kindergarten, and beyond. As the world around us expands through college and our first real work experiences, so do the connections we must form just to function in the modern world.

Our emotional solvency has a direct impact on the quality of our relationships — and the quality of our relationships has a direct impact on our emotional solvency. Indeed, the people we know who are emotionally healthy enjoy generally positive relationships. Conversely, those who don't seem to get along with anyone seem to have a host of emotional issues.

When we love someone, we want to let that person in, emotionally and socially. To do this, we need to create a space for that person. The other, then, exists as a part of our life. There is oneness, but also a sense of separateness. In a relationship, if someone is self-absorbed, there is no room for anyone else. This is why we are quite literally repelled by arrogant people, and attracted to those who are humble and when appropriate put others' needs before their own.

Self-esteem is the foundation of every relationship. When we lack a positive sense of self, our relationships all suffer. And as our relationships decay, so, too, does our emotional wellbeing.

The Gift of Giving

People who give tend to enjoy a positive self-image and personality traits that reflect a healthy emotional state. In fact, research has even shown that certain areas of the brain exhibit elevated levels of activity when a person gives. Giving literally excites the brain; it produces electricity (Krueger et al., 2001).

Some early researchers of altruism and giving believed that egotistical motives and a shallow positive public image were the main driving forces behind our choice to give to certain causes and needs. However, the most recent social research has completely rejected those theories and shown that genuine giving is actually an intrinsic part of the healthiest expression of the human condition (Piliavin & Hong-Wen, 1990).

The more self-esteem we have, the more complete we are. Receiving, after all, is a natural and reciprocal consequence of giving. The cycle of giving and receiving is the perfect union.

When we only take, however, we are left feeling empty and are forced to take repeatedly in a futile attempt to feel complete. Constant taking only reinforces our dependency, and continues to exhaust us emotionally, spiritually, and physically.

A person with high self-esteem has the capacity to give and to love. Every positive emotion stems from giving and flows outward from us to others, while every negative emotion revolves around taking.

Consider, for example, lust versus love. When we lust after someone or something, we think in terms of what they (or it) can do for us. When we love, however, our thoughts are immersed in what we can give to someone else. Giving makes us feel good, so we do it happily. But when we lust, we only want to take. When someone we love is in pain, we feel pain. When someone whom we lust is in pain, we only think in terms of what that loss or inconvenience means to us.

Revisiting Childhood, Again

For the conversational archeologist, there are layers and layers of fossil records to examine. The most telling layer is the foundation layer — the beginning. For example, it is rare to find an emotionally healthy person with considerable unresolved anger toward a parent.

A person who holds onto anger and negative emotions, perhaps due to a traumatic childhood, probably experiences difficulties building positive and meaningful relationships. One might hear from such a person statements like: "You can't trust anyone in authority."

As we delve deeper, pay attention to how he talks about his childhood, parents, siblings, other relatives, childhood friends. A person who speaks harshly of his childhood or relatives — particularly if he uses strong, violent language — clearly has unresolved issues that could potentially result in explosive behavior.

Archaeologists often plan several digs before they eventually excavate the actual bones. As we speak to the individual in question, look for clues beyond what is immediately obvious. The Conversational Archeologist looks for clues that the person unconsciously leaves embedded in her conversation.

No family is without issues, but does she consider hers worse or better than most? Certainly, seeing a person scream and yell at her parents or speak derogatorily toward her elders is a troubling sign, but a general mistrust of authority is also a typical indicator of a difficult childhood.

If someone has one or two people in his life with whom she does not get along well, it's certainly not anything to be concerned over. But if she complains about more than a few people (past and present), and accuses others of treating her unkindly or stabbing her in the back, the reality may well be that *she* is the problem.

No Boundaries, No Limits

Jerry Seinfeld introduced into the lexicon the term "close talker" in his famous hit TV sitcom Seinfeld. The character was a friendly person who, nonetheless, seemed to be completely unaware that there's such a thing as personal space. The close talker stands too close when speaking to us, perhaps touches us when we don't want to be touched—oblivious to our body language.

Each of us has a self-defined force field of personal space, a personal bubble, designed to buffer us from too-close contact with others. When someone invades our space, we feel uncomfortable. While there are many cultural differences regarding what is customary and acceptable space, the boundaries are tacit, but generally understood.

We all know space invaders — people who grossly violate that accepted, albeit unspoken, norm. And that says something about them. If we take a step back or show some other clear sign of discomfort and the person ignores our comfort zone — whether through ignorance or apathy — this is a sign that he is not attuned to the wishes of others, or worse, does not understand, much less appreciate, boundaries. Or worse still, someone who senses our discomfort, but intentionally continues to disrespect our boundaries.

As people become less emotionally stable, boundary problems become more prevalent. And not all boundaries are physical. A poor self-image translates into porous, permeable, leaky boundaries—because if I don't have a clear definition of myself, I'm unable to effectively judge where you begin and I end.

Healthy boundaries are not created to keep people out; rather they exist to define our space and our sense of personal responsibility. In a previous chapter, we saw that the compliant personality is often unable to ask for help, even when it is desperately needed. Furthermore, he is unable to refuse a person's request of help, even if it is unreasonable. He says yes to the endless demands of others, but won't ask someone else for small favors, which will require no longer than five minutes of a person's time. This is the kind of person who freely drops his pennies into the "Take a penny, leave a penny" container, but finds it difficult to *take* a penny.

On the flipside is the arrogant person, who generally has no respect for other people's boundaries. He resists taking responsibility for his own life, so he attempts to control the lives of others. He often pushes the boundaries of others, by persuading, coaxing, or bullying the other person into complying with his desires. Indeed, a lack of shame means that he will ask or demand of others to do things for him that he himself would never do for anyone else—despite all his claims to the contrary.

We should ask ourselves, "Does he respect or violate rules and the rights of others?" We say, "I'm on a diet, please don't bring cake," and she brings it anyway, because she can't show up without bringing something. He says he can fix our computer, and even though we tell him not to, he takes it anyway because he wants to surprise us by fixing it. Minor infractions? Perhaps, perhaps not.

A person with a clear sense of boundaries is willing and able to offer to help others, when such help is understandable and reasonable. And at the same time, he can ask others for help in a responsible, direct, and non-manipulative manner.

Proper Attachment and Disengagement

The pattern of assumed intimacy can be identified as a sign of boundary issues early on in a relationship. People who are ego-driven and/or have grandiose personalities may take liberties with our emotions. They may assert themselves too quickly into a relationship, be it personal or professional.

During our conversation with the person, look for signs that he is getting too personal too quickly. In the beginning of the relationship, did he come on too strong or too fast? Did he become preoccupied with everything we said? While we may be initially flattered, we should ultimately be concerned. If we aren't, we will likely learn the lesson the hard way.

This pattern of disregard for standard relationship etiquette may indicate lack of respect for appropriate boundaries, as well. For instance, let's say that you are the boss and your subject of observation is your employee. The employer-employee relationship has (or should have) clear and well-defined barriers, and crossing those barriers willfully (or disregarding them altogether) is a potential indicator of an ego-driven personality. One sign may be found in the difficulty the employee has in using formal titles—Doctor, for instance—because of a perceived subordinate nature of the relationship.

◆ ◆ ◆

The line between mental health and mental illness can be razor thin and blurry. Still, we seek to quantify our findings. Suppose your new co-worker seems to exhibit a lack of responsibility at times, but can also be, on occasion, thoughtful, patient, and kind. What does this mean?

How much credit does he get for those positive traits, and how many points does he lose for the negative ones? The answer is not so cut-and-dry; but the rest of this book will seek to organize, in a general sense, degrees of stability. While no approach offers perfect accuracy even for professional diagnosticians, the skills we learn will give us a distinct edge in determining the emotional health of others.

SECTION 3

Building the Emotional Profile

CHAPTER 8

The Mental CAT Scan –
The Five-Minute Exchange

People say conversation is a lost art;
how often I have wished it were.

Edward R. Murrow

O ften we see, but aren't really paying attention. We hear, but aren't really listening. Observation is careful, calculated, and purposeful. Having read the previous chapters of this book, it should be easier now to detect low self-esteem in a person by the way he speaks and behaves. We are now aware, for example, that what might appear to be boastfulness or confidence is likely to be a sign of low self-esteem.

In some cases, we may get enough information in those

first few minutes of initial interaction to conclude that the person is emotionally unstable. However, that isn't always the case.

The CAT scan cannot filter out false positives. Consider, for instance, the trait of humility. Remember, self-esteem and the ego are inversely related, so the greater one's self-esteem, the less arrogant one is. But suppose the person we're observing acquiesces to the wishes of others, not because he genuinely wishes to be helpful, but because he's afraid to say no, or does not feel worthy of asserting his feelings. We cannot quickly distinguish between those who are humble and enjoy high self-esteem and those who allow themselves to become doormats.

Let's take another example. A person who seeks attention for attention's sake does not represent the apex of emotional health. However, there are also people who prefer not to blend in, but *need to.* They're afraid of being noticed, and have a tendency to mask surface appearances altogether.

Think of the CAT scan as a colander with large holes. It serves as an initial filter so that anything which gets caught — i.e., anything that doesn't slide through the holes — is surely problematic. However, just because everything gets through the colander doesn't mean that the person is free of any issues.

Be aware that many individuals appear to be very well put-together at first. Not only is their dress normal and appropriate, and their speech free of any glaring indicators of emotional problems, they may also appear to treat people well and respect their personal space. They outwardly appear to be poster children for normal.

Therefore, this person may not appear to exhibit any of the warning signs, but this does not automatically mean he is emotionally healthy. The more socialized a person is, the more adept he is going to be at hiding his flaws.

For instance, narcissists and sociopaths (e.g. con artists) often make very good first impressions. They may initially come across as warm, caring, generous, and even altruistic — if they are socially polished. Consider Ted Bundy, who charmed many unsuspecting women to their death by appearing to be a nice, pleasant gentleman. Had those women been able to spend more time with him, his serious flaws would most likely have begun to surface.

Even the pros can get thrown. In a landmark work entitled *The Mask of Sanity*, Dr. Hervey Cleckley, a clinical professor of psychiatry at the Medical College of Georgia, discussed the difficulties inherent in identifying psychopaths, and attempted to clarify the psychopathic personality.

Although the psychopath's inner emotional deviations and deficiencies may be comparable with the inner status of the masked schizophrenic, he outwardly shows nothing brittle or strange. Everything about him is likely to suggest desirable and superior human qualities, a robust mental health (Cleckley, 339).

Although the above is an extreme example, we will find many people pass the initial screening, but go on to score poorly on the next system, the Conversational Archeologist test. Below are emotional footprints that are generally indicative of mental health issues, and when observed we want to pay close attention to them. Please note that some of these signs may indicate a specific diagnosis, and may not be representative of the person's overall emotional health. For instance, a person who is oblivious to social cues may suffer from Aspergers; and odd or highly idiosyncratic behaviors may be the result of OCD (Obsessive-Compulsive Disorder).

CAT Scan

Level 1: Observation

1. *Lack of Focus:* Very distracted (can't focus, looking around; responding to or noticing every movement or noise) / very fidgety / can't sit still (e.g. constantly moving, may be shaking leg, or constantly picking lint off clothing).

2. *Inappropriate Dress:* Dressed unsuitably for the occasion (e.g. shows up to job interview with low-cut dress

and very short skirt; dressed in winter clothing on a very hot day). Flamboyant dress (very flashy, highly colorful clothing, makeup and hairstyle that is unusually provocative) / highly unusual dress or appearance.

3. *Low Energy:* Low energy / apathetic / negative (appears to move in slow motion; sluggish in speech or movement).

4. *Idiosyncrasies:* Odd or highly idiosyncratic behaviors (e.g. constantly straightening things for no obvious purpose; avoids stepping on cracks; odd, repetitive movements) odd speech, posture, gait – (may speak in a monotone voice – no vocal inflection; posture and / or gait are stiff, rigid, very awkward).

5. *Overly Dramatic or Expressive:* Dramatic / exaggerates / attention-seeking (e.g. person makes a scene, draws attention to self with dramatic behaviors; describes things using a lot of exaggeration; acts in ways to get those around to notice – must be the center of attention).

6. *Lack of Patience/Tolerance:* Highly impatient / overly demanding (e.g. shows little tolerance for having to wait in line – may be tapping fingers or foot, heavy sighing or rolling eyes, irritable if made to wait for only a brief period; expects others to cater to his needs or wishes).

Level 2: Observation

7. *Emotional Disconnect:* Detached / cold (very un-friendly, perhaps somewhat rude, aloof – reluctant to interact but in an unfriendly, rather than shy, manner – does not respond in a warm or friendly manner to others' kindness or friendliness).

8. *Paranoia:* Suspicious (Highly untrusting; eyes may be darting, looking around constantly; may refuse to make casual conversation as if we intend to harm him in some way; overly guarded).

9. *Distressed Appearance:* Poor hygiene / unkempt (un-shaven, appears to not have showered in a few days, messy and dirty hair, clothes rumpled, dirty).

Level 1: In Conversation

10. *Unnatural Communication:* Constantly interrupts / overly talkative (doesn't allow the other person to get a word in; completely dominates the conversation; talks non-stop). May speak very fast, and sound pressured (as if he can't stop – impossible to interrupt him) / volume of speech is loud.

11. *Uneasy State:* Uptight, tense / easily flustered / nervous (person is not calm or relaxed, appears anxious, easily embarrassed).

12. ***Lack of Appropriateness:*** Makes improper remarks or asks embarrassing or highly personal questions in a conversation with someone he barely knows without at least a casual, perfunctory preface or a display of sincere regret afterwards.

13. ***Continual Self-References:*** Grandiose /bragging/ frequent self-reference (e.g. constantly shifting the conversation back to self to talk about his accomplishments or his various wonderful qualities (in his eyes); name-dropping; "one-upping" others in conversation).

14. ***People-Pleaser:*** Too agreeable / fawning / too eager to please / doesn't want to bother anyone (this person always agrees; never disagrees despite what he really feels, believes, or wants; eager to please others by doing anything they want or showering them with flattery).

15. ***Put-Downs and Cut-Downs:*** Belittles others, and is quick to make fun of people, even under the guise of, "just having fun." Enjoys hearing of another's misfortune, and spreading hurtful rumors and gossip.

Level 2: In Conversation

16. ***Socially Unaware:*** Oblivious to social cues and violates others' personal space. This person is unable to read people's responses to his behavior – for example, if he is being inappropriate or too loud and others show

noticeable signs of discomfort, he does not pick up on it; also, he may stand too close while talking.

17. *Sexually Seductive:* Overly flirtatious/ overly familiar with someone just met or barely knows (this person acts flirtatiously or comes on strongly to people he or she just met; he may treat someone as if he already knows them really well even though he just met them; e.g. calls a doctor he sees for the first time by his first name, pats him on the back; hugs people who don't even know him).

18. *Ignores Boundaries:* Doesn't hear "No"/ really pushy, forces opinion (e.g. person offers to do something for us, and he ignores a firm "No thank you," even though it is repeated numerous times. He ignores our clear indication that we are uncomfortable with doing something; and disregards our opinion while pushing his opinion on us; general lack of regard for our wishes).

Final Analysis

Human behavior is too rich and complex to assign a rigid system of assessment, particularly when our interaction is assumed to be limited. The most effective analysis then, is one that allows for us to organize our findings into general categories, rather than a pass/fail scoring.

- In observation alone, or in brief conversation, a person who exhibits two of the footprints in Level 1 *may* suffer from at least minor emotional issues.

- In either observation alone, or in brief conversation, a person who exhibits three or more of the footprints in Level 1 is presenting a fair degree of emotional instability.

- In either observation alone, or in brief conversation, a person who exhibits four of the footprints in Level 1, or one or more footprints in Level 2, warrants attention, and questions of emotional health are likely.

Trait Versus State

In assessing behavior, it is important to distinguish *traits* from *states*. In other words, we want to determine whether someone is behaving a certain way because of who he is at the core, or whether he is simply reacting to a particular situation. A personality *trait* is a characteristic of personality that influences our thoughts, feelings, and behavior. Generosity, shyness, and aggressiveness are all examples of traits. Traits follow us throughout life, which is why they are valuable as predictors of future behavior. They are ongoing aspects of a person, not the result of a particular environmental situation.

A *state*, on the other hand, is a temporary emotional

condition, a reaction to situations and events. Situations may not change our traits, but they can definitely influence how we express our traits — both positively and negatively. Environmental influences can be the spark that ignites temperament. An aggressive personality trait, for example, will lead to more angry states. *But behavior must always be evaluated in the context of the person's current life situation.*

Our assessment cannot come with enough disclaimers! There may be perfectly valid reasons why a person will exhibit a negative indication of mental health — for *any* of the footprints mentioned above. Maybe the person has poor hygiene because he just spent three days helping a friend detox and hasn't yet had a chance to shower and change clothing; or perhaps he has low energy because he just ran a marathon for charity. In any event, investigation is recommended to see if there is a situational cause for his unusual behavior, because it certainly places the person into question mark territory.

For a healthy person to exhibit a level two footprint is also feasible, but there better be a very good reason. Is it *possible* that the seemingly paranoid person is really a CIA operative? Sure. Likely? No. Indeed, a person who brags about a certain aspect of his life may be trying hard to impress us, while one who seems aloof or detached may have been the recipient of traumatic news — and the situation is quite understandably dictating his behavior.

We can see how psychological states can complicate profiling. At times, our emotional responses to situations are temporary states, and once we are removed from the situation, or when circumstances change, our feelings do, too.

The Positive Indicator

Disagreements and conflicts arise when two people are in *constricted consciousness*, where each needs to take, rather than to give, in order to be emotionally nourished. It is impossible to have a productive conversation when two people feel out of control. For instance, arguments may easily ensue when people are worried about something. Why? Because they are dependent on the outcome of a situation about which they feel helpless. (Research that parallels this idea show that patients who are able to control their IV painkiller dispense to themselves less of the drugs, and report feeling less pain. The sense of control alleviates the fear and anxiety that fuels the pain [Chen, 1996]). Therefore, they are unable to communicate properly and give to each other; they are forced to take.

In an anxious or harried state, it becomes increasingly difficult for us to see beyond our own needs, and to look at the situation objectively and rationally. Similarly, a person who is in physical pain may experience difficulty focusing on the needs of others. A migraine headache, for instance, produces a pain we cannot control, and so we may be more easily irked or angered when we find ourselves in such a situation.

Our frustration level increases and our tolerance decreases when we are in a bad mood. Almost anyone can be warm, kind, and generous when he is in a positive state (although if he's not, then consider this a warning sign). *However the true indicator of emotional health is when a person can respond to negative situations with patience and tolerance, even when he is in a low emotional or physical state.*

Moreover, an emotionally healthy person is more likely to see beyond a person's rudeness. His broader perspective enables him to feel compassion and express empathy even in trying circumstances. He also recognizes that whatever is happening is likely not the end of the world. Even if he is disappointed by the turn of events, he does not take it personally or choose to feel victimized.

There is no false-positive here, because even the compliant personality will find it difficult to maintain his patience when in a bad mood. As a *general* rule, when we observe a person behaving in such a way, our assessment of his emotional status is positive.

◆ ◆ ◆

The next chapter outlines footprints that are designed for encounters or relationships with a higher degree of familiarity and interaction.

CHAPTER 9

The Conversational Archeologist

Wise men talk because they have something to say;
fools, because they have to say something.

Plato

W̲e can all be inconsistent in our behavior and react to situations in an unpredictable manner. It is easy to misinterpret these reactions, and attach significance to them when, in reality, even the healthiest person can have idiosyncrasies. Conversational archeology helps to offset such misinterpretation.

The competent conversational archeologist not only knows how and when to ask the right questions, he also knows how to correlate the information he receives with his understanding of the Four Facets.

For example, the insurance industry uses credit rating to determine whether they should offer coverage to someone. Credit score and insurance coverage are not directly linked, but statistics suggest that the healthier your credit history, the less likely you are to file a claim against your insurance policy, and the more likely you are to pay your insurance premiums. If you have a troubled credit history — or little or no credit history — you may pay higher premiums than someone with a better credit history. You may even be denied coverage altogether.

This formula can be extended to behavioral and emotional patterns. For instance, if we know someone who gets his car tuned up regularly and makes sure his oil is changed every three months, it is more likely he also visits the dentist regularly and undergoes regular health check ups. In other words, there is a likely correlation between how responsible he is about keeping his car running smoothly and how well he takes care of his health to ensure his body runs efficiently. Frequent visits to the dentist could suggest a disproportionate emphasis on teeth, but, in general, it's a sign of responsibility.

In order to construct a more accurate profile of the subject, try to construct some questions (or make statements) that don't reveal our intent. Using the previous example, we might say something like, "My friend hates going to the dentist for check-ups and has put it off for so long, he now needs oral surgery. Can you imagine?"

As we engage the person in the topic, he will quite often give us an opinion which reflects his own values. In this case, if he tends to be less responsible, he may jokingly respond, "That sounds like me. I haven't been to the dentist in years!" or, conversely, "That's one of the reasons I make sure to get my teeth cleaned every six months, as I don't ever want to end up with gum problems."

To provide another example, let's say we want to determine whether a person is compassionate or not. As conversational archeologists, we might mention a recent tragic news story and see how she responds. For example, "Did you hear on the news about that family whose son just got back from Iraq and was killed in a car accident on his way home from the airport?" A compassionate person will typically respond empathetically by saying: "Wow, I can't imagine what his parents must be feeling" or "That's horrible! What a tragedy!" On the other hand, someone lacking compassion will typically appear unmoved by the story, shrugging it off with a callous or matter-of-fact statement such as, "Well, life's often not fair."

We can also casually broach sensitive issues, and then use follow-up statements that will help amplify the initial response. The questions shouldn't be too transparent. No one likes to feel like a bug stuck on the end of a pin. Cleverly-worded phrases should offer an unguarded window into the person's thinking. Always be aware of context. Questions should be sandwiched into a typical conversation that would otherwise take place without suspicion.

When we are less direct, mentioning other people or situations, the person's response or reaction will typically reveal an insight into how he thinks. Remember, our goal as conversational archeologists is not to try to diagnose a psychiatric disorder, but rather to create a profile which is reliable enough for us to determine whether or not the person is emotionally healthy.

Just What Is "Normal," Anyway?

Assuming that there are no glaringly obvious indictors of mental illness, such as hallucinations or suicide attempts, clinicians often face a difficult task when trying to draw the line between normal and abnormal. At what point does eccentricity become a disorder?

In general, when a person's behavior begins to cause significant personal distress and impairs his ability to function effectively at home or work, it is safe to conclude that there may be a significant mental health problem. But there are many degrees of distress and impairment.

There's an ago-old riddle that asks: "How far can you go into a forest?" The answer is *halfway*; because after you reach the middle, you're beginning to come out. In gauging emotional wellbeing, we're often looking for the middle of the forest — balance and moderation. When exhibited in the extreme, practically any attitude or behavior, no matter how admirable or reasonable, begins to drift into that gnarly thicket of unhealthy.

For example, cleanliness is a virtue until someone becomes so obsessed with being clean that his behavior becomes compulsive and unhealthy. Demonstrating a degree of openness and receptiveness is a positive and healthy trait, of course; so is being appropriately cautious and reserved. But when we move into the extreme of either of these two traits, we're drifting into questionable terrain.

Dedication to exercise is a positive, healthy attribute; however, running with a broken foot because we feel we must "get our exercise in" is clearly not a good sign. Such extreme behavior places a person in the red zone. Almost any admirable trait has an unhealthy counterpart, as demonstrated with the following examples:

- Being affectionate is positive, while distant or aloof is not—excessively clingy is unhealthy.
- Showing courage is positive, while cowering is not—being brazen is unhealthy.

- Having determination is positive, while being indecisive and unsure is not—close-mindedness is unhealthy.

- Being flexible is positive, while being rigid and stubborn is not—lacking backbone is unhealthy.

- Trusting others is positive, while being paranoid is not—being too naïve is unhealthy.

Therefore, each of the following footprints contains filters to screen out the unhealthy extreme. In assessing our subject, we should check to see that his attitude or behavior is balanced. If he gets caught in the filter, then he would not receive a positive mark for that trait; instead he should be given a -2, or -1 if the expression of the extreme (filtered behavior) is milder.

Conversational Archeologist Scale

Instructions: The footprints are in the form of questions. For each item below, ask yourself how you would describe the person, and then record the score based on the degree to which he exemplifies the *positive* of the trait.

For example, in the first footprint, Integrity, if your subject is someone who almost always conducts himself with a high degree of integrity, then he would receive a +1; if he mostly exhibits the trait, a 0; if only sometimes, a -1; and if rarely or never, then -2. Again, if he scores a +2, but is identified with a filtered behavior, then his score for that trait is changed, and becomes negative (either -1 or -2).

1. **Integrity**: Does he make commitments and stick to them — whether it is keeping an appointment or helping a friend in need? Or does something always seem to come up that interferes with him being able to follow through?

   ACTS WITH INTEGRITY:
   Often/Frequently/Habitually +1
   Mostly/Generally/Typically 0
   Sometimes/Occasionally -1
   Rarely/Seldom/Infrequently -2

   Filter: Is he highly inflexible and unwilling to revise his plans or change his mind when things no longer make sense or become objectively problematic?

2. **Honesty:** Is he a person of his word and can he be trusted? When he borrows something, is it returned in good shape, and without delay; or do you constantly have to chase him down to repay a debt or obligation? Is he careful about the truth, even when it comes at his own expense? Or does he tell lies that advance his personal agenda or take advantage of others?

A POLICY OF HONESTY:
Often/Frequently/Habitually +1
Mostly/Generally/Typically 0
Sometimes/Occasionally -1
Rarely/Seldom/Infrequently -2

Filter: White lies, such as telling his wife her new hairstyle is great, even though he hates it, is appropriate, healthy, and most would argue, smart. Candor or bluntness at someone else's expense, demonstrating little or no sensitivity to pain he is causing, is indicative of a person who lacks empathy and perspective.

3. **Regard for Social Norms:** We all find some rules to be inconvenient, such as outrageously low speed limits on certain roads. Nonetheless, the healthy person generally abides by, even if he doesn't appreciate, the law of the land. Does this person have respect for law and order—structure and civility? Or does he disregard social norms and feel that laws and rules do not apply to him.

RESPECT FOR RULES:
Often/Frequently/Habitually +1
Mostly/Generally/Typically 0
Sometimes/Occasionally -1
Rarely/Seldom/Infrequently -2

Filter: One who is afraid to bend or break even the most minor rules because he fears the consequences has a disproportionate or excessive fear of authority.

4. **Personal Responsibility.** Does he pay his credit card bills on time, and live within his means? Or is he careless or irresponsible with his money? Is he thoughtful and calculating in his decisions? Or does he engage in high-risk behaviors (unprotected sex, gambling, etc.), demonstrate poor judgment, and is reckless with his own safety and that of others? Does he think things through and consider the consequences? Or would he be described as someone who makes rash or impulsive decisions?

Is He Responsible?
Often/Frequently/Habitually +1
Mostly/Generally/Typically 0
Sometimes/Occasionally -1
Rarely/Seldom/Infrequently -2

Filter: A person who is miserly and denies himself or those in his care the most basic of necessities fosters an unhealthful attitude towards money. Growth means taking chances. If this person is so paralyzed by fear that he is unable to make smart and calculated decisions — afraid to live and equally afraid to die — then he has drifted into negative territory.

5. **Interpersonal Responsibility:** Does he attempt to be well-mannered and polite to everyone, or is he rude or condescending to those he deems "unimportant," such as the waiter, the taxi driver, or the store clerk? Does he only lavish attention on those who he considers to be on his social level or higher?

RESPECT FOR ALL:

Often/Frequently/Habitually +1

Mostly/Generally/Typically 0

Sometimes/Occasionally -1

Rarely/Seldom/Infrequently -2

Filter: The compliant type is the quintessential people-pleaser, at the expense of his own dignity and self-respect. Can he politely but firmly speak up when his food is undercooked at a restaurant, or does he meekly eat it without saying a word? Does he tolerate being treated badly? A healthy person is one who can speak up when necessary and say no to favors asked of him when he is disinclined to give.

6. **Emotional Core:** A person with healthy self-esteem is swayed neither by excessive praise or criticism. Does he take things in his stride, or does he take offense easily, always making everything about him? Is he quick to misread or misinterpret the behavior of others? Does he overreact to perceived insults, slights, or criticism? Is he a person of reasonable patience, or does he easily lose his temper and become disproportionately angry over minor setbacks?

LET'S LITTLE THINGS GO:
Often/Frequently/Habitually +1
Mostly/Generally/Typically 0
Sometimes/Occasionally -1
Rarely/Seldom/Infrequently -2

Filter: For all intents and purposes, there is no filter here. A person who is able to remain calm, regardless of the situation, is operating on a high emotional level. In extreme instances, a person who does not react emotionally, whatsoever, to even the most egregious offense, including his own objectionable behavior, may suffer from a type of serious pathology that does not allow for him to experience genuine emotion.

7. **Perspective:** Does this person have a balanced outlook on life's priorities? Or does he blow little things out of proportion, while perhaps ignoring the major things? Would you say that he knows what is important and what is not, or does this person live in a perpetual state of chaos and crisis, where there is always something going on—and he routinely turns to others as his solution.

BALANCED OUTLOOK AND PERSPECTIVE:

Often/Frequently/Habitually +1
Mostly/Generally/Typically 0
Sometimes/Occasionally -1
Rarely/Seldom/Infrequently -2

Filter: Having faith and optimism that things will work out for the best is certainly healthy. However, a person who remains indifferent to any of life's challenges may not be fully engaging in life, and may suffer from depression or other emotional illness.

8. **Approach to Physicality**: Is this person someone who appreciates looking neat and nice, but recognizes that one's appearance is not reflective of his self-worth? Or is he overly self-conscious and preoccupied with his image and how others perceive him? Does he make a big deal out of a perceived or minor flaw or become very uncomfortable or upset if he doesn't look perfect?

UNCONSUMED BY PHYSICALITY:

Often/Frequently/Habitually +1

Mostly/Generally/Typically 0

Sometimes/Occasionally -1

Rarely/Seldom/Infrequently -2

Filter: A person who expresses absolutely no interest whatsoever in maintaining his physical appearance may be suffering from any number of a range of emotional issues. Dressing modestly with minimal attention to one's physical appearance is positive; neglecting oneself at the expense of one's dignity is not.

9. **Attitude:** Does he have an attitude of gratitude or expectation? Is he a constant blamer and complainer, or is he generally content and satisfied with his proverbial lot? Does he enjoy life despite the occasional setback? Or is he just waiting for the next disaster to happen?

ATTITUDE OF GRATITUDE:

Often/Frequently/Habitually +1

Mostly/Generally/Typically 0

Sometimes/Occasionally -1

Rarely/Seldom/Infrequently -2

Filter: An expansive or elevated mood (where the person shows no restraint in expressing his feelings or is unusually elated) may indicate an unstable emotional state. It is natural to feel highs and lows—the degree and frequency of those extreme emotions makes all the difference.

10. **Self-Expression:** Is the person modest in appearance, speech, and conduct, or is he flamboyant and egotistical, offering anyone who will watch and listen a front-row seat of his talents and accomplishments?

ACTS WITH MODESTY AND HUMILITY:

Often/Frequently/Habitually +1

Mostly/Generally/Typically 0

Sometimes/Occasionally -1

Rarely/Seldom/Infrequently -2

Filter: If the person is forced by fear or coerced by threat into any changes in dress or lifestyle, then his behavior is not considered to be a free-will choice, and is not indicative of either independent thinking or emotional freedom.

11. **Boundaries:** Does this person have a clear sense of appropriate behavior, given the relationship? Does he make unreasonable requests of people he meets for the first time or barely knows? Does he believe in reciprocating or does he prefer to do the taking? Does he respect or violate rules and the privacy and rights of others?

GOOD SENSE OF BOUNDARIES:
Often/Frequently/Habitually +1
Mostly/Generally/Typically 0
Sometimes/Occasionally -1
Rarely/Seldom/Infrequently -2

Filter: A healthy person should be able to solicit help, where appropriate, rather than let a sense of pride or embarrassment — a function of the ego — stand in the way. A person who tells you not to call a doctor or ambulance when he experiences chest pains because he "doesn't want anyone to make a big fuss over him," is not coming from a rational place.

12. **Relationships: Past and Patterns** Does he have several good friends who have been in his life for several years rather than just several short-term or fleeting friendships? How does he talk about his family? His siblings? His parents? Does he take responsibility for any relationships that have soured or do they all seem to evaporate into bitter disappointment and resentment?

POSITIVE, HEALTHY RELATIONSHIPS:
Often/Frequently/Habitually +1
Mostly/Generally/Typically 0
Sometimes/Occasionally -1
Rarely/Seldom/Infrequently -2

Filter: One must let the evidence speak for itself, rather than rely exclusively on the person's own description of his relationships. Certain individuals are "best friends" with the world and love everyone, and wrongly assume that everyone loves them in return. Such a person has a grandiose and flawed perception of how they are viewed by others.

13. **Empathy or Envy:** A person is generally in either of these two camps. A lack of empathy and a tendency to be envious are two major signs of emotional instability. Can he put the needs of others ahead of his own? Can he feel happiness for someone else, even when he's having a difficult day or going through a hard time? The ability to rise above our own problems and focus on the welfare of another is a sign of emotional health. Of course, we all are, to some extent, self-absorbed, particularly when we're struggling with personal challenges. But the intensity and duration of this self-absorption is particularly revealing.

Empathy Over Envy:

Often/Frequently/Habitually +1
Mostly/Generally/Typically 0
Sometimes/Occasionally -1
Rarely/Seldom/Infrequently -2

Filter: A person's extreme sensitivity to the pain of others may be the result of an inability to identify with his own pain; therefore, being ensconced in the pain of others serves as a surrogate to his own suffering, and an escape from healthy introspection.

14. **Live and Let Live:** Does he find it extremely difficult to recover from a rejection? If a person is unable to let go, or even worse, seeks revenge, it may be a sign of emotional volatility. How quick is he to apologize when he is wrong or hurts others? Is he able to forgive when he has been hurt? Those who can easily move their ego out of the way and forgive and apologize where necessary and appropriate, operate with a higher degree of emotional strength.

APOLOGIZES, FORGIVES, AND MOVES ON:
Often/Frequently/Habitually +1
Mostly/Generally/Typically 0
Sometimes/Occasionally -1
Rarely/Seldom/Infrequently -2

Filter: As the saying goes, "Fool me once, shame on you. Fool me twice, shame on me." Being able to forgive and moving on with one's life is healthy. However, ignoring repeated abuse and offensive behavior is an indication of low self-esteem. The person does not love or value himself enough to assert and protect himself.

Final Analysis

As stated in the previous chapter, the most effective analysis allows for us to assess the person, and then structure our findings with flexibility, rather than rigidity. Therefore, our analysis is designed to offer a general insight into a person's emotional framework, rather than confining him to a specific illness or diagnosis. Furthermore, the test is designed to be simple-to-use, without complicated calculations that would make casual assessment, impractical.

Normal is not a trend. It's not a passing fad or the latest popular group-think about how people should behave. Normal is far more slippery to pin down. But that's okay. We don't have to be able to chart a formal multi-axial diagnosis to know a strong deviation when we see it.

- A person of extreme emotional health will have a score of + 3 or higher and will not demonstrate any of the extreme behaviors (– 2 or filter traits) described in the categories above.
- A person of fairly sound emotional health will have a score of –1 to +2 and will not tend to demonstrate any of the extreme (– 2 or filter traits) described in the categories above.
- Many of us are somewhat neurotic—we might even say that a little neurotic is the new nor-

mal. Therefore, a person who exhibits one or two of these footprints in the extreme (– 2 or filter traits) may still be within the realm of average—even though the behaviors are arguably unhealthy. The score for the average person is –7 to – 2.

• If many of the behaviors that best describe our person under observation are consistently negative, and to a greater degree, we are most definitely swimming in questionable waters. A person who scores – 8 to – 12 is suffering from at least mild emotional issues.

• A score of less than – 13 indicates a great likelihood of poor emotional health and it is probable that this person is suffering from an emotional illness.

◆ ◆ ◆

The analysis presumes, however, that no white or red flags are evident. The following chapter discusses what signs will automatically move any person into negative territory.

CHAPTER 10

The Alarm Bells

Freud: If it's not one thing, it's your mother.
ROBIN WILLIAMS

I n the clinical world, danger is a relative term. Yes, danger can signify a physical threat, but more often, the word will denote a potentially toxic relationship that adds stress and complication to our lives. It is important to be aware that the sounding of alarm bells does not indicate that this person is malicious or sinister. Anyone who suffers with an emotional illness is deserving of our complete compassion and kindness. And if the person who is exhibiting this behavior is a family member or a close friend, the best way to be of assistance to a loved one is to seek professional help.

The Flags: Hazard Versus Out-of-Bounds

Throughout this chapter, our warning signs will conform to the flag system that golf courses use to mark boundaries. In golf, boundaries are marked by red flags and white flags. Red flags indicate a hazard and a one-stroke penalty. White flags indicate an out-of-bounds scenario and a more significant penalty.

The object of the profiling game is to spot flags and identify the degree of hazard attached. Each time we build a profile, we'll be looking for flags and asking ourselves: Is this particular behavior a mild hazard (red flag) or clearly out-of-bounds (white flag)? Here's an illustration of a red flag versus white flag situation that we may encounter.

Your friend has asked you to go somewhere you don't want to go. You've already said "No," but the friend keeps pushing you to say "Yes." His behavior could indicate one of two possibilities:

Red Flag

He just wants you to get out of the house, experience something different, and take a small risk for a bigger gain (or so he says). If this is the case, maybe he is going too far, but his pushiness is not indicative of a major problem.

White Flag

The second possibility — refusing to take no for an answer — can signify a white flag. As Gavin Debecker, noted security consultant and author of *The Gift of Fear* (1997), points out, when someone refuses to hear the word "No" it can be a really strong indicator that we're in danger. When someone ignores our "No," he is seeking control of the situation, or refusing to relinquish control. Every situation is different. But if a person categorically discounts our wishes and simply steamrolls over our objection without acknowledging our feelings, we have a white flag situation.

As we have stressed throughout this book, *there will always be gray areas*, and some alarm bells will ring louder than others. But there will also always be alarm bells that rings so loud that they can be heard from outer space.

Let's look at some more clear-cut examples of hazardous versus out-of-bounds behavior. Consider the case of a person who cannot tolerate frustration or disappointment and is prone to outbursts of aggression and violence whenever an argument ensues. A person who continually comes unglued at the slightest mention of something disagreeable, or frequently engages in violent behaviors like hitting and throwing objects, may have finally gone out of bounds.

Another example: consider the person who prefers solitude and demonstrates little interest in maintaining relationships.

While introspection and self-discovery are very healthy — there are spiritually-evolved individuals who retreat into long periods of solitude — such anti-social behavior cannot be considered the norm. A tendency to maintain distance can be considered a hazard, but when the behavior moves further and further into the realm of the strange and eccentric, the person may be heading for the out-of-bounds line, especially if he begins exhibiting abusive behavior (which comes with its own hazards and out-of-bounds flags).

If the person is verbally abusive in any way, be aware that physical abuse is, statistically speaking, not far behind. While it is possible that the abuse will not become physical, the odds are against it. And verbal abuse can be as emotionally damaging as physical abuse to the person on the receiving end. It's a white flag in the making.

Similar situations are common in the workplace, as well. Does a co-worker act like a loner? Is he slightly hypersensitive, or is he embroiled in troubled relationships with other co-workers? A person who doesn't get along well with others may only be an example of a red flag, perhaps harmless. Still, as we begin to learn more about this person's personal life and extracurricular activities, we may realize that his behavior does indeed indicate a white flag.

If someone seems particularly frustrated by his workplace conditions and refuses to tolerate what he deems to be unfair and unjust treatment, pay attention. It's a red flag, until we collect more evidence. A person like this may be dangerous — a white flag may be on the horizon.

What we'll often find is that our initial observations will reveal red flags, but conversational archeology and a little time may show that those red flag are, in actual fact, really white flags.

Multiple Hazards

In many cases, a red flag may be harmless. But combine it with two or more other red flags and it quickly becomes a white flag situation. Has the person recently suffered a financial or personal crisis, such as a bankruptcy, separation, or divorce? Has she ever endured a restraining order, custody battle, or some other domestic court hearing? If she's already exhibiting red flag behaviors, one more source of stress or pain could push her over the edge, and ultimately be cause for concern.

Any red flag, when accompanied by low self-esteem, can quickly escalate into a white flag situation. Is the person becoming increasingly frustrated because he can't seem to move up the corporate ladder? If he has always struggled with low self-esteem, the situation can quickly escalate from a red flag to white flag situation. Someone who keeps talking about being fed-up or sick and tired of everyone and everything has now slipped into the black-and-white terrain of absolutes, and several red flags may be flying all at once.

Substance abuse is an obvious white flag, but people often differ on how many drinks equals abuse, or which drugs are considered to be non-addictive prescription drugs, soft drugs, or dangerous narcotics. But this much is certain: If several people are discussing their concerns about someone who has already ignored continual suggestions to dial it down, this person has already passed the red flag zone and has entered the white flag zone.

Disturbing behavior, such as neglecting oneself, allowing mess to accumulate, avoiding the dentist, and forgetting appointments, can eventually shift someone into the red flag zone.

Reckless risk-taking often emerges out of such a hazardous situation. As we discussed earlier, this person may attempt to manufacture happiness, and devise artificial means of feeling alive, such as using drugs, driving recklessly, sleeping around, or shoplifting. One red flag has now turned into two or more, and we clearly have a white flag situation. One red flag may not be enough to make a judgment call, but several issues combined will always escalate the situation from hazardous to out-of-bounds.

Finally, there are the neon-flashers which are screaming *Out-of-Bounds*. Self-mutilation, excessive use of drugs and alcohol, and careful planning of suicide are all unquestionably white flags. Serious talk of injuring others, especially when in retaliation for an offense that revolves around a lack of respect (whether perceived or real), is also considered to be a definite white flag situation. No need to look for additional hazards in these cases. This person is already way out of bounds and requires professional help.

Rule 27

If you're a golfer, you know about Rule 27 — the lost ball scenario. We think we might have hit a great shot, but we just can't find our ball. Where did it go?

Often, in the game of life, we have a friend who has strayed into the trees and has landed in a hazard, or has possibly even gone out of bounds. We may be required to accompany our friend off the fairway and into the tall grass to look for what has been lost. There we will search for his ball, hoping it hasn't gone out of bounds. At the same time, we begin to wonder to ourselves: *How crazy are we to be spending all we time out here chasing a lost golf ball, when we need to get back to our own game?*

Golf's Rule 27 actually handles this predicament well. Under the penalty of one stroke (similar to a psychological white flag situation), we hit another ball as close as possible to the spot from which the original ball was first played. In other words, we start over and proceed under penalty, as in the case of an out-of- bounds scenario. It's a provisional shot, designed to help players navigate an unclear situation.

It is difficult to know where to draw the line when assessing if a person's actions are emotionally unstable. The flags we are about to explore will serve as guidelines for discovery, rather than definitive markers. We are looking for *degrees* of stability (or instability).

Psychosis is more concerning than neurosis — psychosis is a three-alarm flag, while neurosis, depending on the severity of the symptoms, will generally only be a two-alarm or one-alarm flag. As we discussed earlier, most people are slightly neurotic, but most of us aren't slightly psychotic.

What's the difference between neurosis and psychosis?

Think of neurosis as anxiety, insecurity, and irrational fears. People with neurotic tendencies have difficulty adapting and coping to change, and are generally incapable of developing a rich, complex, and satisfying personality. Neurotic tendencies can manifest as depression, anxiety disorders (e.g. OCD, phobias, social anxiety disorder), and even personality disorders, such as borderline personality disorder or obsessive-compulsive personality disorder.

Psychosis, on the other hand, is a break with reality, characterized by deranged personality, delusions, and hallucinations. (We'll take a closer look at psychosis as we discuss how it manifests itself in white flag behaviors.)

Psychological disorders are often classified as either *ego-dystonic* or *ego-syntonic*. Behaviors, thoughts, or feelings that upset a person and make him uncomfortable are ego-dystonic. He doesn't like them, he doesn't want them, and that makes him more inclined to seek treatment for his troubled behavior.

But often personality disorders are ego-syntonic: from that person's perspective, his thoughts, behaviors, and feelings are all parts of his identity. Even if everyone else believes that he is suffering from a disorder, he refuses to accept the reality, and will operate under the assumption that everyone else has the problem, not him. And if he believes that his behavior is normal and acceptable, it is unlikely he will seek treatment.

Renowned psychiatrist, Dr. Thoman S. Szasz, sums up the distinction succinctly and amusingly: "Those who suffer from and complain of their own behavior are usually classified as neurotic; those whose behavior makes others suffer, and about whom others complain, are usually classified as psychotic" (Szasz, 1974).

Flags Guide

Below is a composite overview of warning signs. Each is ranked by severity: three-alarm flags are the strongest indicators of emotional insolvency, while one-alarm flags are less concerning.

Please keep in mind that this book is not an academic treatise, nor is it meant to be used as a diagnostic tool. What follows is not an exhaustive list of every psychological disorder with all the formal criteria that clinicians would use to diagnose each disorder. Rather, the flags described below may be thought of as a guide to assessing general emotional solvency—even though they are grouped according to category.

The white flags provide a foundation that will help us become more attuned to the signs of emotional instability and help us in determining the risk factors associated with forming a relationship with our subject. As well, perhaps, they may serve as a catalyst to getting ourselves or loved ones the appropriate help, should we find these indicators hit closer to home.

White Flags: Three-Alarm

Three-alarm flags communicate the message: *something is not right.* Any individual who exhibits these behaviors is in urgent need of immediate professional help.

Delusional Thinking — Unchanging, irrational beliefs that have no basis in reality. In the extreme form, the person may exhibit grandiosity, claiming that he is some sort of celebrity, god, or prophet (e.g. Charles Manson). Such grandiosity could be indicative of disorders such as psychosis, narcissism, or severe mania. Delusional individuals are often highly introspective and preoccupied with fantasy. Does the person hold unusual beliefs, such as *magical thinking*? These beliefs will influence their behavior. For example, does the person often see causality in coincidence? For example, he honks his car horn and the traffic light "magically" turns green. Stressful experiences and trauma can impel people toward magical thinking.

Many people are slightly superstitious, but this person's life may be ruled by beliefs that have no basis in fact. He has, to some degree, lost the ability to distinguish between what he can control and what he cannot. The correlation between cause and effect is distorted.

Psychosis — A break with reality; schizophrenia is an example of the most extreme psychotic behavior. Psychosis occurs when the person loses contact with reality; he hears, smells, or feels things that others can't detect (hallucinations); and strongly believes things that are known to be false, such as being certain that he is a king or that the devil is speaking to him.

Persecutory delusions are most common; the person typically believes she is being tormented, tricked, ridiculed, or followed, or suffer from thought broadcasting, thought insertions, and delusions of control. For instance, the person may have thought insertions such as "My thoughts are not my own." Or thought broadcasting: "Other people can hear my thoughts."

Psychosis can also occur within the context of other disorders (e.g. severe depression, postpartum depression). These psychotic features can be either *mood-congruent* (for example, a depressed man feels so guilty that he imagines he has committed some heinous sin) or *mood-incongruent* (for example, a depressed woman believes she is being persecuted by the CIA).

Mood-Congruent psychotic features include delusions or hallucinations that are consistent with the typical depressive themes of personal inadequacy, guilt, disease, death, nihilism, or deserved punishment. Delusions of guilt may, for example, drive the individual to decide that he is responsible for the death of a loved one. Delusions of deserved punishment could include believing that one is being punished for some moral transgression. Disease delusions might include believing that one has cancer, or that one's body is rotting away. In a person suffering from depression, hallucinations are usually transient, and not as elaborate as the hallucinations of people with full-blown psychosis (e.g. schizophrenics).

Dissociation — A disintegration of the normally integrated functions of consciousness, memory, identity, or perception. This disturbance may be sudden or gradual, transient or chronic. In its least severe forms, it might manifest as phasing out (short periods of altered consciousness similar to a blackout), or as short-lived episodes of amnesia. Multiple Personality Disorder is an example of severe dissociative behavior, where the personality splits into multiple personalities that live distinctly different lives (e.g. Sybil).

Suicide Attempts or Gestures — What is the difference between a *suicide attempt* and a *suicidal gesture*? A suicidal gesture is when a person may go through the motions of attempting to commit suicide, but in reality, has no intention of dying. For example, the person may take a non-lethal dose of sleeping pills or cut himself in such a way that the wound is unlikely to cause imminent death. The suicide gesture is generally intended to express despair or helplessness or to utter a cry for help in an effort to improve one's life, rather than to die. In some cases, a suicide gesture may be an attempt to make a dramatic statement or "get even with someone." Such behavior most commonly occurs among people with personality disorders, such as Borderline Personality Disorder.

A suicidal attempt may be a failed suicide. For example, a person may ingest a bottle of pills with the intention to kill himself, but someone intervenes, calls an ambulance, and the person wakes up alive in the hospital, having had their stomach pumped. Others may intend to die but choose a method that is unlikely to bring about the desired result. For example, a person may drive a car off a steep cliff, certain that she will be killed, but somehow manages to survive the wreck.

Suicide attempts and gestures can look a lot alike. Either way, it's a white flag situation, and the person needs professional help. Gestures may eventually become attempts, and attempts may eventually be successful.

The fact that someone is in crisis does not necessarily mean she is on the brink of suicide. These warning signs will help you evaluate the risk:

- Talking about feeling suicidal or wanting to die
- Feeling hopeless that nothing will ever change or get better
- Feeling helpless that nothing one does makes any difference
- Feeling like a burden to family and friends
- Feeling extreme, chronic fatigue, coupled with depression
- Abusing alcohol or drugs
- Putting affairs in order (e.g. organizing finances, giving away possessions, visiting friends or family members one last time)
- Organizing a plan for suicide (e.g. method, date)

- Buying instruments of suicide (e.g. gun, rope, medications)
- Writing a suicide note
- Intentionally putting oneself in harm's way, or in situations where there is a danger of being killed (e.g. "suicide by cop").

Some people are at higher risk for suicide than others. People who are at higher risk include those who suffer from the following illnesses:

- Major depression, Bipolar Disorder and/or Substance-Abuse Disorder or other serious mental disorders such as psychotic disorders or personality disorders (e.g. Borderline Personality Disorder)
- Stressful life events combined with other risk factors, such as depression. Stressors might include divorce, separation, bereavement, chronic illness, medical condition, or loss of job. (See the *Holmes & Rahe Stress Scale* in Chapter 12 for more.)
- Previous suicide attempt or gesture
- Family history of mental disorder or substance abuse

- Family history of suicide
- Family violence, including physical or sexual abuse
- Firearms in the home (guns are used in 50 percent of all suicides)
- Incarceration
- Exposure to the suicidal behavior of others, such as family members, peers, or celebrity figures
- No social support system (e.g. family, friends)

Violence — In assessing whether or not someone is violent, here are some white flags to look for:

- This person talks seriously about injuring others, especially if the offense was a lack of perceived or real respect.
- This person appears to be callous and unconcerned about how his behavior makes other people feel. He doesn't experience guilt or learn from his mistakes, even after he has been punished or detrimentally affected. He tends to blame other people for his problems or constantly finds excuses to rationalize and justify his behavior.

- This person is given to thinking obsessively about a subject without being able to let go; often these thoughts will be of a sexual or violent nature.

- He cannot tolerate frustration and is prone to outbursts of aggression and violence.

- He is characterized by emotional instability and an inability to control his impulses, with episodes of threatening behavior and violence occurring, particularly in response to criticism by others.

White Flags: Two-Alarm

It's a sign of the times that some of the behaviors below do not warrant three-alarm status:

- **Paranoia** is an unwanted and unjustified feeling that others are trying to harm you. Is the person overly suspicious? Does she often misconstrue the friendly or neutral behavior of others as unfriendly or hostile? Mild paranoia might manifest in the form of someone believing that she is being talked about behind her back, and that she is constantly being insulted.

- **Self Harm and Self-Mutilation** — A deliberate infliction of physical injury to the self without intention of dying (e.g. cutting or burning). For example, a person might intentionally use a knife, razor, or broken glass to make what are known as small cuttings to the skin to cause bleeding. More extreme cutting might be a suicide gesture.

Narcissistic Personality Disorder

Symptoms of narcissism include:

- Grandiose sense of self-importance (e.g. he exaggerates achievements and talents, and expects to be recognized as superior without commensurate achievements)
- Preoccupation with fantasies of unlimited success, power, brilliance, beauty, or ideal love
- Belief that he or she is special and unique and can only be understood by, or should associate with, other special or high-status people (or institutions)
- Requiring excessive admiration
- Sense of entitlement, i.e., unreasonable expectations of especially favorable treatment or

automatic compliance with his or her expectations

- Interpersonally exploitative, i.e., takes advantage of others to achieve his or her own ends
- Lack of empathy: unwilling to recognize or identify with the feelings and needs of others
- Frequent envy of others or the belief that others are envious of him or her
- Strong display of arrogant, haughty behaviors or attitudes

Clearly, in the case of someone who has Narcissistic Personality Disorder, lack of empathy is more than just a minor side effect of low self-esteem. If we identify in someone a decided lack of empathy and resulting attitudes of extreme envy and a sense of entitlement, it's an indication that there's more beneath the surface.

Borderline Personality Disorder

Emotions and behavior are poorly regulated in borderline personalities, due to their often devastatingly low self-esteem. Consequently, they usually act anxious, depressed, irritable, or bored.

They desperately fear abandonment. Does she continually attempt to latch onto us, and punish us if we fail to live up to her expectations? She may be a borderline personality. Borderlines typically also suffer from comorbid moderate to severe depressive episodes.

Symptoms of borderline personality disorder include:

- Frantic efforts to avoid real or imagined abandonment
- A pattern of unstable and intense interpersonal relationships characterized by alternating between extremes of idealization and devaluation
- Identity disturbance: markedly and persistently unstable self-image or sense of self
- Impulsivity in at least two areas that are potentially self-damaging (e.g. overspending, sex, substance abuse, reckless driving, binge eating).
- Recurring suicidal behavior, gestures, or threats, or self-mutilating behavior
- Affective instability due to a marked reactivity of mood (e.g. intense episodic dysphoria, irritability or anxiety, usually lasting a few hours and only rarely more than a few days)
- Chronic feelings of emptiness
- Inappropriate, intense anger or difficulty controlling anger (e.g. frequent displays of temper, constant anger, recurrent physical fights)

• Transient, stress-related paranoid ideation or severe dissociative symptoms

Attention Everyone: Histrionic Personality Disorder

Everyone has a personal style of display, and we can glean insights into a person's emotional health by determining what motivates him to present this image to the rest of the world.

Doing something for the sole purpose of drawing attention to oneself is a sign of emotional imbalance. If we seek to feed off others in any way, we will become emotionally unwell. We relegate ourselves to a position of dependency, and by extension, we become increasingly self-centered and vulnerable. We're setting ourselves up for neurosis/anxiety and depression.

The desire to garner attention is not limited to appearance. Histrionic Personality Disorder (HPD), for instance, is characterized by excessive emotionality and attention-seeking.

A person with this disorder is generally highly functional, so we might not suspect a problem if we were to judge her based on her career or family status. She may be socially and professionally successful, but also be manipulative in order to remain at the center of attention.

Symptoms to look for include: exhibitionist behavior, excessive dramatics, constant approval-seeking, extreme sensitivity to criticism, inappropriate seductive behavior, the need to be the center of attention, low tolerance for delayed gratification, and rash decisions.

Notice whether the person is uncomfortable in situations where she is not the center of attention. How does she interact with others? Does she tend to exaggerate her emotions and is she attracted to drama and intrigue?

A mnemonic that can be used to remember the criteria for HPD is **PRAISE ME** (Pinkofsky, 1997).

P =   provocative or seductive behavior

R =   relationships, considered more intimate than they are

A =   attention, which she must be at center of

I =   influenced easily

S =   speech style — they want to impress and their speech lacks detail

E =   emotional shallowness

M =   make up of physical appearance, often used to draw attention to themselves

E =   exaggerated emotions and theatrical presentation

Interestingly enough, a person with special attributes (such as an especially attractive particularly creative person) may have built an identity around those gifts, but may, in reality, suffer from low self-esteem. It is conceivable that such a person received praise and positive feedback all her life on account of the gifts she was born with, so she never invested much effort into developing herself in other ways. It is important to remember that confidence and self-esteem are separate psychological entities.

Red Flags: One-Alarm

Mood Disorder

Do you observe signs of depression? Psychological (mental/emotional) symptoms of depression may include:

- Persistent low mood
- Low self-esteem and low self-confidence
- Pessimism and negative outlook
- A sense of despair
- Hopelessness and helplessness; feelings of worthlessness
- Thoughts of suicide
- Irrational feelings of guilt

Depressives also typically suffer from anhedonia, or loss of pleasure, in activities they used to enjoy. Somatic (biological and physiological) symptoms may include:

- Fatigue and lack of energy
- Inability to concentrate or make decisions
- Sleep difficulties; either too much or too little sleep
- Sexual dysfunction, such as loss of sex drive
- Change in appetite, weight gain or loss
- Psychomotor activity changes, such as slower movements or speeded up, agitated movements

Bipolar Disorder Flag

Does the person's mood swing from euphoric highs to the depths of despair? We may be observing episodes of mania mingling with depression. Manic (or hypomanic) behavior is confident, positive, cheerful, optimistic — even euphoric. A person with bipolar disorder is friendly with the world, bubbles with creative ideas, and embarks on ambitious new projects (that are rarely finished). Then the mood swings the other way, and the person becomes depressed, frustrated, and perhaps irritable and angry.

Bipolar disorder is characterized by unusual and severe mood changes that cycle from extreme highs (mania) to extreme lows (depression) and sometimes, back again, with periods of normal mood in between. Severe changes in energy and behavior accompany these dramatic mood swings.

People with bipolar disorder experience both manic

episodes (or hypomanic episodes) and major depressive episodes, and in some cases, mixed episodes — which includes symptoms of both mania and depression.

The mood states in bipolar disorder can be viewed as a spectrum or continuous range of states. At one pole is severe depression, above which is moderate depression, then mild, short-lived depression. In the middle of the spectrum lies normal or balanced mood, above which is hypomania (mild to moderate mania), and at the top (the second pole) is severe mania.

Symptoms of mania include:

- Grandiosity or exaggerated self-esteem
- Reduced need for sleep (e.g. feels rested after only a few hours of sleep)
- Increased talkativeness, rapid speech, pressure to keep talking
- Flight of ideas or racing thoughts
- Easily distracted; i.e., attention too easily drawn to unimportant or irrelevant external stimuli
- Speeded-up psychomotor activity or increased goal-directed activity (social, school or work)
- Poor judgment and excessive involvement in pleasurable activities that are self-destructive, for example: spending sprees, sexual indiscretions, foolish business investments

Manics are often inclined to share their jolliness with others. Their humor may even be quite infectious, but as the mania worsens, that humor becomes less cheerful — it begins to take on a driven, unfunny quality that makes others uncomfortable. An inflated ego can become grandiose to the point of delusional; for example, manics may believe they're qualified to advise presidents or solve global crises such as world hunger.

Manics are usually unaware that their behavior is inappropriate. They often deny that anything is wrong, rationalizing that a person who feels good and is productive cannot possibly be ill. But they can create difficulties in the lives of all those who interact with them.

Anxiety

Anxiety disorders are characterized by: 1) the presence of anxiety; and 2) the avoidance behaviors calculated to ward it off. While each anxiety disorder has different symptoms, they all cluster around excessive, irrational fear and anxiety, apprehensiveness, and dread. And the sufferer develops avoidance behaviors, such as ritual acts or repetitive thoughts to protect himself from experiencing the anxiety.

We all feel anxious from time to time, and a certain level of anxiety is normal — even adaptive. For example, if we're about to take a test, the fear of failure will motivate us to study hard. But excessive anxiety can be terrifying, paralyzing, and debilitating. Fear and uncertainty begins to dominate and torment the lives of people suffering from anxiety disorders. Severe anxiety wreaks havoc on relationships, and interferes with career and family responsibilities on a daily basis.

General symptoms of anxiety (Generalized Anxiety Disorder, in particular) include:

- Feeling wound-up, edgy, tense, or restless
- Tiring easily
- Difficulty concentrating
- Irritability
- Increased muscle tension
- Trouble sleeping (initial insomnia or restless, unsatisfying sleep)

CHAPTER 11

Statistically Speaking

There is no great genius without some touch of madness.
Seneca

There may be a near-infinite number of behavioral variables, but statistics can help us in assessing a person's emotional health. If we flip a coin 100 times, the statistical probability is that we'll get 50 heads and 50 tails. In the same way, if we take a random sampling of human facets and footprints, odds are, we will draw certain basic conclusions.

Every clinical researcher deals with this concept of sample size and how results normalize with a population of a certain size. In a nutshell: The higher number of trials (in this case, experiences) we have, the more concrete and reliable our results will be. In examining a large sampling of flips (in our case, humans), we can identify statistical patterns.

Research identifies four major statistical factors that can be used to indentify whether a person's emotional health is likely to tilt in one direction or the other. The list is neither comprehensive nor definitive, but it can be a useful tool in our assessment.

1. Psychiatric Conditions Genogram
2. Marital Status
3. Religious Beliefs
4. Creative Leanings

Psychiatric Conditions Genogram

Genograms can help chart an individual's family psychological history, including both psychiatric illnesses and the emotional-relationship dynamic within the family. Ideally, it is preferable to ask the person these questions openly and directly, but when that's not possible, clever conversational archeology will help us gather information and form correlations. If an opportunity presents itself, it's helpful to speak to the person's family members to gain a broader perspective.

1. Has he ever been diagnosed with any psychological disorders, however brief? Was he ever hospitalized for this disorder?
2. Does any first-degree relative in his family have a history of mental health problems?
3. Has he ever attempted suicide or had serious suicidal thoughts?
4. Is he addicted to alcohol, drugs (prescription drugs), or any other substance?

Are Married People Happy and Healthier?

Marriage indicates a profound degree of emotional health if the couple in question enjoys a close relationship and the marriage has been maintained for a long time.

Research conducted by University of Chicago researcher and professor of Sociology Dr. Linda J. Waite showed that, for both women and men, marriage lengthened life and substantially boosted physical and emotional health. Marriage (as opposed to couples who simply lived together) also raised income over that of single or divorced people, and was shown to increase each spouse's sense of control.

In the 1972 publication of *The Future of Marriage*, Jessie S. Bernard reported that married men are better off than single men in four measures of psychological distress: depression, neurotic symptoms, phobic tendencies, and passivity.

Married women also scored better on these negative traits than single women.

Generally speaking, married people report statistically fewer signs of psychological distress and higher rates of emotional wellbeing than unmarried or divorced individuals. A study following 14,000 American adults over a ten-year period found that marital status was one of the most important predictors of happiness. Married Americans were more than twice as likely than divorced or separated Americans to say they were very happy with life in general.

Research conducted by Brigham Young University professor, Julianne Holt-Lunstad, suggests that marriage may literally be a matter of the heart. Studies revealed that happily married adults have lower blood pressure (about 4 points lower) than singles who have supportive friends. And unhappily marrieds have higher blood pressure than both happily marrieds and singles. If our blood pressure dips during sleep, we're at much lower risk for cardiovascular problems than those whose blood pressure remains high throughout the night (Holt-Lunstad, Birmingham & Jones, 2008).

These studies also showed that spouses help to balance people in their lives and make them generally healthier. Spouses help to temper others' moods, soften their rough edges, and give people perspective on the harsher aspects of the world.

While a troubled marriage may not raise a red flag or white flag, it can be an eventual contributor to other aspects of emotional instability which can become red or white flags in themselves (e.g. depression and anxiety).

In God We Trust

Religious commitment has been associated with a decreased prevalence of depression, and there remains an indisputable correlation between involvement with religious activities and emotional health. As W.A. Black has stated in his *An Existential Approach to Self-Control in the Addictive Behaviors:*

> Religious commitment may also be related to a lower incidence of substance abuse. Numerous studies have linked alcohol and other drug abuse to a lack of purpose in life, which is often associated with low levels of religious involvement. Larson and Wilson demonstrated this religious void in their study of the religious life of alcoholics. When surveying a group of alcoholics about their religious histories, the researchers discovered that 89% of the alcoholics had lost interest in religion during their teenaged years, whereas among the control group, 48% had an increased interest in religion and 32% had remained unchanged.

Creative Genius or Mad Genius?

Creativity is perhaps one of the most intricate topics surrounding normality. The complex personality constellation of many creative individuals serves as an effective reminder of why we should be careful not to judge anyone. Creative people have made tremendous contributions toward the betterment of humanity and offer sheer genius to the world's repository of masterpieces. Vincent Van Gogh, Ernest Hemingway, Abraham Lincoln, and Winston Churchill are just a few examples of creative geniuses who suffered from severe depression. Despite the handicap of mental illness (or perhaps *because* of it), they went on to make a difference in the world.

Previously quoted author of *The Mask of Sanity*, Dr. Hervey Cleckley, writes: "Unusual and apparently irrational behavior has indeed been so commonly reported in the lives of those acclaimed as great artists and thinkers that there is a popular tendency to regard it as the rule rather than the exception."

A person may be extremely successful in his career and public accomplishments, but that does not mean that he is easy to get along with. It's one thing to admire Winston Churchill for saving the world from destruction but another thing entirely to live with him. It's widely known that Churchill's family members struggled with his excessive drinking. Though he had an optimistic perspective in his earlier years, pessimism later emerged. The dark side of his character became even more obvious after he left public office, but those character traits didn't suddenly appear. They had always been brewing beneath the surface, even during his years as a statesman and promoter of optimism. In public, these individuals are heroes. But in private, they are often conflicted individuals who lead pained existences.

In the Stanford Report of 2002, researchers published the most conclusive evidence about the link between creative genius and mental illness. The results were discussed by Kate Melville in a subsequent article where she explained that creative individuals had a much higher rate of manic depression (bipolar disorder) than the general population.

Healthy artists were shown to be more similar in personality to individuals with manic depression than they are to healthy people in the general population. The leading research manager in Stanford's Department of Psychiatry and Behavioral Science's Bipolar Disorders Clinic explained it in the following way:

> My hunch is that emotional range, having an emotional broadband, is the bipolar patient's advantage . . . It isn't the only thing going on, but something gives people with manic depression an edge, and I think it's emotional range.

Although creative individuals are certainly worthy of admiration and appreciation, many also tend to display extreme moodiness and neuroticism as part of a core of characteristics that researchers have dubbed "negative-affective traits." These traits also include mild, nonclinical forms of depression and bipolar disorder.

This paradox is often depicted in pop culture. In movies such as *A Beautiful Mind*, the story is told of Nobel laureate John Nash, who was both a creative genius and a severely mentally ill person. Movies that depict historic figures individuals often omit key flaws that might not be so well received by the viewing public. The protagonist, after all, must be a character that audiences can empathize with, and the more heroic, the better.

In the movie, Nash pays tribute to his wife Alicia in his Nobel Prize acceptance speech. In reality, however, Nash was not asked to give a Nobel lecture, presumably because of his instability. He did, however, give a short speech at a small party in Princeton. In the real speech, he remarked that he was not inclined to give speeches, but that he had several things to say. First, he hoped that getting the Nobel Prize would improve his credit rating because he really wanted a credit card. Second, he said he knew that one is supposed to say one is glad to be sharing the prize, but that he wished he'd been the only winner because he really needed the money badly. Such comments might be humorous when hearing them on television, but when you learn the details of the real life that plagued this individual, the laughter subsides.

The traits below outline some characteristics of mentally ill geniuses that are often identified by researchers (*Handbook of Creativity*, published by the Cambridge University Press):

- Openness to experience, especially fantasy-oriented imagination
- Impulsivity, lack of conscientiousness
- Anxiety, affective illness, emotional sensitivity
- Drive, ambition
- Nonconformity, norm-doubting, independence
- Hostility, aloofness, unfriendliness, lack of warmth

Creative people are often able to generate remote and seemingly unrelated associations between separate ideas, indeed, across disciplines. Their thinking may defy linear or logical progression. In creative pursuits, such independent thought may sometimes have its advantages but, in the daily experience of life, it can become a tiring burden.

Highly creative individuals are often inclined to exhibit above-normal levels of symptoms associated with clinical diagnosis. Examples include introversion verging on withdrawal, depression, manic episodes, and seemingly antisocial behavior.

Perhaps the most challenging aspect of having a relationship with such individuals is the fact that no amount of statistical evidence will convince them that the problem lies with them. Creative genius has the distinctive quality of making its own rules, and nowhere is this more evident than in the case of someone who comes to believe that he is, in fact an island unto himself.

In Summary

Are we saying that a highly creative, never-married, atheist, who has suicidal thoughts and addicted to drugs, is definitely emotionally unstable. No, but statistically speaking, the odds are not in your favor.

CHAPTER 12

The Resilience Factor

In order to succeed, people need a sense of self-efficacy, struggle together with resilience to meet the inevitable obstacles and inequities of life.

ALBERT BANDURA

Modern research has shown us that psychological disorders result from a combination of factors — genes, neuro-chemistry, environment, personality, and other developmental factors. We come from diverse gene pools and different environments. We have distinct physiologies and chemistries. We have each experienced different stressors throughout our lives, and we have developed varying levels of emotional resilience to cope with those stressors.

The phrases *emotional resilience* and *psychological resilience* are tossed around interchangeably. Both point to the capacity to adapt to and cope with stress, and to overcome adversity without becoming psychologically dysfunctional such as slipping into a persistent negative mood or true clinical depression.

Resilience can be thought of as emotional Teflon-coating. It is a kind of hardiness that not only helps us cope with the everyday stresses of life, but also protects us when we're confronted by significant stressors or traumas in the future.

Stress can sneak up on us. Stressors can pop up without warning, and sometimes, unfortunately, all at once. What qualifies as a stressor? Anything we consider to be threatening to us in some way, either physically or emotionally. Actual stress only occurs when we have doubts about our ability to deal with that stressor. Starting a new job, for example, can be stressful because we aren't yet convinced we can do the job. In other words, stress only becomes a problem when we lack the resources to cope with it.

In one form or another, stress contributes to most psychological and physical health problems. That being said, stress doesn't necessarily leave us with a permanent dent. As the saying goes, that which does not break us makes us stronger; and research, and perhaps your own life experience, bears this out.

Stress becomes dangerous when it interferes, for an extended period of time, with our ability to function normally. For example, we may find ourselves feeling out of control and powerless to fix even relatively minor problems. These feelings of helplessness can cause us to feel continually fatigued, unable to concentrate, or irritable.

When we build a profile of someone, it is important to always factor in their current, previous, or impending stressors, and evaluate their resilience factor. How well do they hold up under stress?

Our ability to maintain self-control largely dictates our level of calm or anxiety. After we make a poor choice, the dissonance between reality and ego widens — we start trying to justify our choice, which only further torques the ego. In much the same way that a virus or common cold taxes our immune system, stressful situations tax our emotional immunity and can even rock our emotional core. A startling 75 to 90 percent of all physician office visits are for stress-related ailments and complaints.

Over time, chronic stress consumes more energy resources than our body can produce. Stress directly impacts our neuroendocrine stress pathways, changing our body's nervous system and hormone levels, and ultimately weakening our body's natural ability to cope with emotional stress and physical illness.

Stress triggers our body's built-in response mechanisms; for example, have you ever found yourself sweating because you were about to miss a critical deadline? This reaction is caused by hormones that help our bodies cope with threats and uncertainties. This is not entirely bad, because that physiological reaction can motivate us to act and give us that extra boost of energy necessary to get us through the day. The problem is that the longer our mind feels stressed, the longer our physiological reaction systems remain activated —our body gets stuck in crisis mode, which can lead to serious health problems.

While stress doesn't guarantee physical illness, it certainly increases the risk. And stress can diminish a person's ability to recover from illness. People who have suffered heart attacks, for example, tend to have a much harder time bouncing back if they're also experiencing major stressors, such as financial worries or alcohol abuse. On the other hand, the ability to effectively cope with stress can significantly accelerate recovery from a heart attack.

We know that stress plays a major role in triggering and worsening cardiovascular disease, cardiovascular disease, osteoporosis, inflammatory arthritis, type 2 diabetes, some (e.g. viral) cancers and infectious diseases. Stress literally attacks every cell in our bodies (Cohen, 2007).

Every cell contains a tiny clock called a *telomere*, which

shortens each time the cell divides. Short telomeres have been linked to diseases such as HIV, osteoporosis, heart disease, and aging. The telomerase enzyme within each cell keeps immune cells young by preserving their telomere length — that is, their ability to keep dividing and generating new cells (Effros, 2008).

The stress hormone cortisol suppresses immune cells' ability to activate telomerase, which may explain why the cells in people under chronic stress have shorter telomeres. When the body is under stress, it boosts production of cortisol to support our fight-or-flight response. Elevated cortisone levels, however, wear down the immune system.

Short-term stress actually revs up the immune system — an adaptive response that prepares our bodies for injury or infection. But long-term or chronic stress causes too much wear and tear, and the system breaks down. When the emergency stress response is triggered, the body quickly mobilizes all its resources for action. Functions that are not on the emergency team temporarily shut down. When hormones are raging — preparing for battle — energy-consuming components of the immune system, such as white blood cell production, are temporarily suppressed.

The good news is that we can significantly impact our body's response to stress by, for instance, manufacturing more natural killer cells (called T-cells). These amazing fighting units have the ability to recognize and selectively kill cancer cells and virus-infected cells. Researchers have actually measured variations in T-cell activity based on subjects' interactions between stress and attitude. Dr. Steven Locke at Harvard Medical School questioned subjects about stressful events in their lives and their psychiatric symptoms of distress. He found that the T-cell activity level of the group with high stress and low symptoms was *three times higher* than those with high stress and high symptoms.

In other words, people who suffer from high stress, yet have the tools to deal with it, actually have greater immunity than those who have lower stress levels but poor coping skills. Our bodies can withstand living with daily stress. But in order to remain emotionally and physically healthy, we must be able to manage it.

How Men and Women Process Stress

In assessing a person's stress level, it is important to be aware that men and women sometimes respond to stress differently and may thus exhibit different symptoms.

The fight-or-flight stress response in men is sometimes characterized as "tend-and-befriend" in women. Males confront a stressor either by overcoming or fleeing it, whereas women may have responded by nurturing offspring and affiliating with social groups.

The difference in how men and women respond to stress is actually neurological. In fMRI studies of stress tests at the University of Pennsylvania School of Medicine, men showed increased activity in the right prefrontal cortex (analysis and decision-making), whereas women showed increased activity in the limbic system — the emotional part of the brain. And the changes last longer in women, which may help explain why the rate of depression and anxiety disorders is twice as high in women (Wang, 2001).

Sometimes optimism can be a simple but effective cure. Maintaining an optimistic outlook reduces the risk of health problems and helps us recover from a major life stressor. Finnish workplace studies of 5007 employees have found that the increase in sick days taken after a major life event was smaller for those who scored higher on optimism questionnaires than with those with low optimism scores (Kivmaki, Vahtera & Elovainio, 2008). Sick leave is often considered to be an indicator of whether a person will retire early due to disability, and can predict whether there's a higher likelihood of cardiovascular disease, cancer, alcohol-related illness, and suicide.

Having pessimistic expectations increases our vulnerability and susceptibility to both mental and physical illness, which may be explained by the fact that pessimists tend to cope with stress by detaching themselves from emotional events, rather than actively engaging in problem-focused coping. Those who have low resilience often find themselves worn down and adversely affected by life's stresses. But those with high resilience have learned the art of self-renewal; not only are they able to cope well with severe stressors, they actually experience those stressors as learning and growth opportunities.

For instance, one person who loses her job might sink into a helpless depression, while another might see it as an opportunity to reinvent herself, and even embrace the change and challenge.

Certainly developing effective problem-solving and decision-making skills can boost a person's resilience factor, but it's also important to build a strong social support system (family, friends, work colleagues, community organizations).

The Life Change Scale

Whether that change is a new job or being served with divorce papers, adjusting to a new situation requires a great deal of energy and good coping skills. Most of the stressors we encounter throughout life fall into one of six basic categories:

- **Acute time-limited or brief stressors.** A public speaking engagement or a job interview
- **Stressful event sequences.** A major disaster such as the death of a spouse or the US ter-

rorist attack of September 11, 2001 — events
that create a series of new challenges, but will
eventually end

- **Chronic stressors.** Pervasive, recurring demands that force us to change our role or behavior and have no clear endpoint; e.g. caring
for a terminally ill family member or coping
with a chronically depressed spouse

- **Distant stressors.** Traumatic experiences that
occurred in the distant past but still have emotional and cognitive consequences, such as
childhood abuse

- **Background stressors.** Traffic jams, loud mu-
sic playing in the background while we're trying to conduct a phone conversation

When we're confronted with a stressor that threatens our
stability, we appraise the situation to decide whether it is
manageable or whether it is beyond our coping resources.
Coping is any strategy we use to deal with a situation that
strains or overwhelms our emotional or physical resources.
Generally, coping strategies fall into one of two categories:
problem-focused coping or *emotion-focused coping.*

In problem-focused coping, you deal directly with the
stressor to change it or eliminate it; for example, you confront

your husband directly about the long hours he's been working and the toll it is taking on the marriage. Problem-focused coping works best when the stressor is controllable; in other words, we can actually do something to change the situation — either change or eliminate the stressor.

In emotion-focused coping, we try to change the way we feel about the stressor. For example, when our boss is critical of our performance, we may not cry or scream at him because we need to keep our job. But we might seek emotional support from empathetic friends and co-workers.

Technically, there's a third category of coping: *avoidance coping.* Common avoidance tactics include denial, distraction, sedation, or numbing (e.g. through drugs, alcohol, overeating). As we have seen, this approach has a fairly low success rate and ultimately tends to only cause more stress.

Research shows that individuals with high life change scores (indicating that they are experiencing multiple changes in their lives at one time) are more likely to fall ill. But perhaps most surprisingly, studies reveal that illness correlates with *any type of change.* In other words, whether the change event is positive or negative is irrelevant to the level of stress we experience.

The circumstances are largely irrelevant; it's the ability to feel in control that is paramount. This phenomenon explains why some people engage in self-destructive behavior even when things are going well. It's not about the circumstances — it's about feeling a loss of control and lacking effective coping skills that would help them manage change.

The *Holmes and Rahe Stress Scale* measures the relationship between significant life changes and stress. To take the test, add the scores for each life event that applies to the past year of your life. The final score provides a rough estimate of how stress impacts your health.

Adults

Life event	Life change units
Death of a spouse	100
Divorce	73
Marital separation	65
Imprisonment	63
Death of a close family member	63
Personal injury or illness	53
Marriage	50
Dismissal from work	47
Marital reconciliation	45
Retirement	45
Change in health of family member	44
Pregnancy	40
Sexual difficulties	39

Gain a new family member	39
Business readjustment	39
Change in financial state	38
Change in frequency of arguments	35
Major mortgage	32
Foreclosure of mortgage or loan	30
Change in responsibilities at work	29
Child leaving home	29
Trouble with in-laws	29
Outstanding personal achievement	28
Spouse starts or stops work	26
Begin or end school	26
Change in living conditions	25
Revision of personal habits	24
Trouble with boss	23
Change in working hours or conditions	20
Change in residence	20
Change in schools	20
Change in recreation	19
Change in [religious] activities	19
Change in social activities	18
Minor mortgage or loan	17
Change in sleeping habits	16
Change in number of family reunions	15
Change in eating habits	15

Vacation	13
[Religious holidays]	12
Minor violation of law	11

Your score shows your level of risk for illness. Scores are ranked as high, moderate, or slight risk of illness. A score of 300 or higher equals a high risk of illness. A score of 150-299 equals moderate risk of illness — a 30% reduction from the high risk category. A score of 150 or less equals only a slight risk of illness.

A modified scale has also been developed for non-adults:

Non-Adults

Life Event	Life Change Units
Getting married	101
Unwed pregnancy	92
Death of parent	87
Acquiring a visible deformity	81
Divorce of parents	77
Fathering an unwed pregnancy	77
Becoming involved with drugs or alcohol	76
Jail sentence of parent for over one year	75
Marital separation of parents	69

Death of a brother or sister	68
Change in acceptance by peers	67
Pregnancy of unwed sister	64
Discovery of being an adopted child	63
Marriage of parent to stepparent	63
Death of a close friend	63
Having a visible congenital deformity	62
Serious illness requiring hospitalization	58
Failure of a grade in school	56
Not making an extracurricular activity	55
Hospitalization of a parent	55
Jail sentence of parent for over 30 days	53
Breaking up with boyfriend or girlfriend	53
Beginning to date	51
Suspension from school	50
Birth of a brother or sister	50
Increase in arguments between parents	47
Loss of job by parent	46
Outstanding personal achievement	46
Change in parent's financial status	45
Accepted at college of choice	43
Being a senior in high school	42
Hospitalization of a sibling	41
Increased absence of parent from home	38
Brother or sister leaving home	37

Addition of third adult to family	34
Becoming a full fledged member of a [religious institution]	31
Decrease in arguments between parents	27
Decrease in arguments with parents	26
Mother or father beginning work	26

A score of 300 or more equals high risk, 150-299 equals moderate risk, and 150 or less equals only slight risk of illness.

Assessing Resilience: The 16 Factors

When we think of resilient famous people, Nelson Mandela and Anne Frank spring to mind. But resilience can be seen in ordinary people on any given day.

Emotional resilience can be a strong indicator of both short-term and long-term stability. A lack of emotional resilience can indicate that the person is eventually headed for emotional instability, especially if he is confronted by severe life stressors in the future. How do you assess someone's psychological resilience? Here are sixteen characteristics that high-resilients generally have in common:

1. Does the person recover or bounce back quickly after hard times?

2. When stressed, does he manage anxiety effectively?

3. Is he able to come to terms with grief or loss without sinking into depression?

4. Does he engage in harsh self-criticisms or dwell on negative self-images?

5. Does he have a "where there's a will, there's a way" attitude when faced with perplexing problems?

6. Does he adapt well to change? Does he seem able to develop coping strategies and apply them to new situations?

7. Does he treat problems as opportunities, especially in times of adversity or loss?

8. Does he take care of his physical health?

9. Does he make realistic plans and take decisive action?

10. Does he have a healthy social support network (a significant other, family, friends, work colleagues)? Does he have close, positive relationships with family members, friends, and others? Is he willing to accept help from them?

11. Does he have confidence in his own strength and ability to cope with adversity, whether independently or with assistance from others?

12. Does he have good communication and problem solving skills?

13. Following a crisis, does he persevere, navigate through the fallout? Can he keep the problem in perspective and not view crises as insurmountable problems? Does

he immediately kick into problem-solving gear? Can he look beyond the present and focus on how he can make his future circumstances better?

14. Does he have self-control? Can he control his behavior when he has strong feelings and impulses?

15. Can he accept change? Can he make peace with what he can't change and restructure goals that are no longer realistically attainable?

16. Is he constantly, perpetually, moving toward his goals?

If we fail to observe at least some of these qualities in the person we are evaluating, odds are pretty high that he lacks emotional resilience. Even if he seem to be able to keep things together now, he may eventually be headed for inner turmoil, if he is confronted by severe life stressors in the future. For low-resilients, sometimes it only takes one straw to break the camel's back.

It's important to understand that resilience is a dynamic quality, not a permanent capacity. Building resilience is a personal journey and we all have the capacity within us to become more resilient.

CHAPTER 13

Family Ties: Is It All in the Genes?

*Longevity, like intelligence and good looks and health
and strength of character, is largely a matter of genetic heritage.
Choose your parents with care.*

EDWARD ABBEY

R obert Ressler, the FBI behavioral scientist who coined the term "serial killer," stated in his book, *Whoever Fights Monsters,* that a startling 100 percent of serial killers were abused as children, either through violence, neglect, or humiliation. Although there is absolutely no certainty that a victim of abuse will become an abuser, it is, statically speaking, more probable that he (rather than a person who was not a victim) will hurt another person in a similar way.

But did these serial killers inherit their murderous psychopathy? Did they inherit an antisocial personality gene? Or was the cause familial, not genetic — environment versus genes? Or both?

These days, it's popular to blame our genes for all our psychological problems, and when it comes to disorder and disease, certainly our genes are not blameless. But do genes really seal our fate? Are we inevitably doomed (or blessed) to become our parents, with the exact same natural talents, intellectual abilities, diseases and disorders that they have? The answer is a resounding *no*.

Genes don't guarantee our destiny, but they do have a say in who we become. Genes influence potential, possibility, probability. But so do environment, personality, culture, geography, experience—and most importantly, choice.

The nature-versus-nurture debate rages on. The best scientific minds and millions of research dollars are devoted to calculating the degree to which our genes contribute to who we are and the degree to which we're molded by our environment.

The answers are seldom black and white. As you gather information about someone's family, it's important to bear in mind that history — whether genetic or familial — is only one indicator, and it must be viewed in context with everything else that's going on in the person's life.

When scientists study the relative influence of nature and nurture, they're trying to pinpoint how much of human nature is inherited — genetic. *Heritability* is the degree to which variation in a particular trait within a certain group stems from individual genetic differences.

Why are some people smarter than others? Why are some people schizophrenic and others aren't? Why do some people who have had a seemingly easy life develop depression and anxiety, while others who've endured hardship after hardship survive and even thrive? Nature-nurture studies can help us explain or predict differences between groups of people, but they don't necessarily help us predict why *individuals* do the things they do.

Thanks to the Human Genome Project (HGP), we now have the complete map of all human genes. A *genome* is the full complement of an organism's genetic material (DNA sequencing) — the blueprint for building all the organism's structures and directing all the processes necessary to sustain the organism throughout life.

Every cell in our body contains DNA (deoxyribonucleic acid), the chemical compound that contains the genetic instructions on how to make us. DNA consists of two long chains of nucleotides twisted into a double helix which is held together by hydrogen bonds. The precise sequence of these nucleotides — the *genes* — determines the characteristics we inherit. A gene is one sequence of DNA that occupies a specific location on a chromosome and determines your individual characteristics — from the color of our eyes to our propensity for developing a particular illness. DNA self-replicates, copying genetic information to each new cell each time a cell divides, which is how we're able to make billions of new cells throughout our lives, yet remain fundamentally the same person.

We humans have around 30,000 distinct genes residing on our 23 chromosome pairs. And while we are all different individuals, the genetic variation between any of us and Albert Einstein is actually less than 1 percent. But inside that narrow 1 percent differential we would find an untold number of intellectual differences — not to mention physical and psychological variations.

While we are all of the same species, our genes have slight variations in structure, and these variations cause differences in our characteristics. Gene variations help explain why even members of the same family who may look alike and share other common characteristics are dramatically different in other significant ways, which could include, for instance, psychological disorders or diseases.

Certain gene variations make us more vulnerable to certain maladies, others protect us from disorders. Some rare genetic diseases are caused by variations in a single gene, but most common diseases are caused by a mixture of several gene variations and external factors, such as stress or toxic substances.

Is Emotional Resilience Genetic?

Why do stressful experiences cause depression in some people but not in others? Several important genetic studies have found that a single gene called 5-HT T can moderate the influence of stressful life events on depression; in other words, a person's genetic makeup may help determine how much impact stress has on him.

The 5-HT T gene produces a protein that modifies a nerve cell's use of the chemical messenger serotonin, which is involved in regulating mood. (This is the protein that is inhibited by antidepressant medications.) 5-HT T has two variant forms, long and short. The short version of the gene has been linked to depression and anxiety. The long variant has been linked to emotional resilience.

The long and short of it is that 5-HT T predisposes some people to depression, and protects others from it. People with either one or two short genes are likely to become depressed in response to multiple stressful experiences like death, divorce, or assault, but — and this is important — they don't become depressed as long as they don't experience severe environmental stressors. In people with two long variants of 5-HT

T, stress did not trigger depression, even if, for example, they had been severely mistreated in early childhood or suffered financial loss, poor health, or deaths in the family.

In the predisposed, early trauma and subsequent adversity lead to depressive symptoms and subtle changes in the brain. Chronic depression produces marked changes in the brain. Certain structures begin to shrink or show structural disorganization. Resilience factors — perhaps including the protein produced by the 5-HT T gene, as well as conscious thought and behavioral modifications — can mitigate that damage or allow for repair.

If you're hoping that you're one of the lucky ones who have two long genes, your odds are around 30 percent. Research thus far indicates that about 70 percent of us have at least one short 5-HT T gene, which may help explain why so many of us are vulnerable to depression. But we also know that depression emerges from the interaction between genes, choice, and experience.

Other genes have been linked to depression, anxiety, and resilience, and more genetic links will no doubt be discovered in the future. For example, researchers have identified gene variants that affect the expression of a signaling molecule called neuropeptide Y (NPY) that is known to be triggered by stress. NPY's release interacts with opioid compounds to help reduce anxiety and relieve pain. And NPY effects appetite, weight control, and emotional responses.

People with the gene variant yielding the lowest NPY levels react with heightened emotion to stressful stimuli, which further explains why people vary in their resiliency to stress (Goldman, 2008).

Flipping the Switch

Throughout our lives, genes express themselves or turn on and off. Some genes are only expressed or "turned on" in response to stimuli from the outside world — environmental influences, lifestyle, and geography. Like light switches, genes must receive electricity to turn on and express their particular proteins. So yes, genes create risk factors, but by themselves, they simply make proteins.

Scientists have even identified specific genes and pathways that are affected by lifestyle and geography. These environmental factors can play a powerful role in turning genes on or off. People who share the same genetic makeup but live in different environments may express genes differently. For example, our respiratory genes are up-regulated or turned on more frequently in urban environments than in rural ones. The genes of urban dwellers, after all, must contend with greater pollution, which can contribute to respiratory diseases that the body naturally tries to ward off.

Studies that assess aspects of child-rearing such as physical punishment, hostility, lack of respect for the child's point of view, and unjustified criticism or humiliation provide another example of the gene-environment interaction. One Notre Dame study of male teens in a juvenile detention center investigated whether a gene associated with dopamine was more likely than a negative maternal parenting style to cause depression. The result? Neither factor alone predicted depression, but the boys who had especially rejecting mothers *plus* a certain form of the dopamine transporter gene were at higher risk for major depression and suicidal ideation (Cummings, 2006).

The Connection Between Genes and Personality

What about the interaction between genes, personality, and temperament? Thanks to *imaging genomics* (e.g. MRI and fMRI), we can study the workings of the brain in a way that helps us understand the genetic mechanisms underlying diversity in human temperament and personality.

Beyond your genetic inheritance and environmental influences, there's another factor at work: the unique, individual, personal *you*. Anyone with children will tell you how different each of their biological children are, even though they are raised in the same environment. In fact, it's often said that parents of one child believe that upbringing determines personality, but parents with two children believe in genetic tendencies.

What connects our genetic inheritance to environmental

experiences? One connection is personality, which is also subject, in part, to genes. Genes influence personality, and personality influences gene expression. Genetic predispositions interact with circumstances to produce unique individuals.

But here's something else to take into account: People are drawn to particular environments because of their personalities. An extrovert may prefer to spend her Saturday night partying; an introvert may prefer to curl up in front of the fireplace with a good book.

Research shows that the same genes that predispose us to depression and anxiety can also make us more sensitive to negative environmental events and even increase our risk of experiencing negative events. Remember the 5-HT T gene? In addition to its link to depression and anxiety, the short variant of 5-HT T has also been linked to the personality trait neuroticism, which provoked some in the media to dub 5-HT T "the Woody Allen gene." (Neuroticism is the tendency toward hand-wringing anxiety, instability, moodiness, and negative thinking.)

Here's another example. Nine different variations of the RGS2 gene have been associated with shy, inhibited behavior in children, introverted personality in adults, and increased activity in the amygdala and the insula, which process fear and anxiety. People with these RGS2 variants are at higher risk for anxiety disorders (Smoller, 2009).

Many psychologists organize personhood or human personality traits into five dimensions, known as the Big Five: *Extroversion, agreeableness, conscientiousness, emotional stability, and openness to experience.* The thinking is that when we describe someone's personality, what we're actually doing is unconsciously taking a measure of these five traits and crunching them together.

Emotional stability and conscientiousness appear to be directly related to physical and emotional wellbeing and longevity; in other words, wellness is linked to changes in these traits over time. Several studies have suggested that three traits — extroversion, neuroticism, and openness to experience — can explain the heritability of life events. People who are extroverted and open to new experiences are more likely to experience positive and controllable life events, whereas people who are neurotic are more likely to experience negative life events — perhaps, in part, because they come to expect them.

When we're trying to pinpoint whether variation within a particular population can be explained by genetic differences between individuals, we have to sort characteristics carefully. Nature and nurture can look a lot alike, and the personality variable always complicates matters.

People with similar personalities seek out similar experiences and may tend to take similar risks. For example, people who seek out excitement might be more inclined to participate in risky activities, which puts them at greater risk for getting into trouble, having serious accidents, getting sick, or other events that provoke depression and anxiety. Someone who is impulsive and prone to alcohol addiction is more likely to end up in bar fights than someone who has neither of these characteristics.

Over the years, much research has focused on how the novelty-seeking personality trait (impulsive, risk-taking, exploratory, thrill-seeking) relates to various psychological disorders. For example, those with high novelty-seeking characteristics are far more likely to become alcoholics, especially if they have an alcoholic parent. On the other hand, people with low novelty-seeking characteristics have a much lower risk of becoming alcoholics.

Someone with an aggressive, impulsive personality is also more likely to end up in bar fights. An "aggression" gene called MAOA is believed to influence how the brain gets wired during development. MAOA enzymes break down key mood-regulating chemical messengers, most notably serotonin. MAOA has two known variants that influence aggression and impulsiveness: the violence-related L version and its counterpart, the H version, which triggers less enzyme activity, thus leaving higher levels of serotonin in the brain (Pezawas, Meyer-Lindenberg & Drabant, 2005).

By itself, the L variant of this gene is likely to contribute only a small amount of risk in interaction with other genetic and psychosocial influences; in other words, MAOA-L doesn't necessarily make people violent. But studying its effects in a large sample of average people allows scientists to evaluate the heritability of aggressive personalities — how this gene variant biases the brain toward impulsive, aggressive behavior.

These predispositions don't necessarily have to be conscious or voluntary. A brawny kid is more likely to be chosen for the football team than a short, skinny kid and might end up being better at the game, not necessarily because he's a better player than a short, skinny child, but because he has more opportunity to develop his skills.

Many studies have shown that the heritability of many psychological traits — from intelligence to depression and anxiety — increases as we mature. This might seem counterintuitive at first, since we tend to think that genes heavily influence and mold us in early childhood. But here's the reason: As we get older, our capacity to determine our circumstances increases and we are more likely to choose environments that reinforce our natural personality tendencies — for better or worse. And those environments influence our mental health, for better or for worse.

Exactly How Risky Is "Genetic Risk"?

Remember, statistics are always simple summaries about similarities amongst a group of people — they don't take into account all our individual characteristics, or any individual we may be evaluating. Gene scans can't tell us with certainty whether or not we will develop a particular mental health disorder. We don't yet know all the possible gene variations which may contribute to — or protect us from — mental health disorders. And we can't necessarily measure the degree to which other factors (e.g. environmental factors) contribute to disorder, or prevention of that disorder.

To illustrate how genes factor into emotional health, let's explore statistics on genetic risk factors for some of the common mental health disorders we're likely to encounter.

Depressive Disorders

Statistically speaking, Major Depressive Disorder is 1.5 to 3 times more common among first-degree biological relatives (DSM-IV-TR). Children, siblings, and parents of people with severe depression are much more likely to suffer from depression than are members of the general population. But the interaction between genetic predispositions, stressful life events, and our individual experiences play a role in causing depression, especially in women. Studies of depression suggest that genes play a greater role in contributing to depression in women than in men (NIMH, 2001). Research suggests that genetic predispositions may be more likely to impact women's sensitivity to stressful life events, making them more susceptible to depression.

Family members do share common neurochemistry, but environment plays a huge role in causing depression, too. First-degree relatives live in the same household, share common beliefs and values, and are subject to the same stressors. When one family member suffers from severe clinical depression, other family members suffer; for example, they may withdraw and become socially isolated, which can contribute to depression later in adulthood.

Higher familial risk has been associated with more severe, recurrent, or psychotic forms of major depression. For example, a child who grows up with a severely depressed parent may feel, or in fact be, socially ostracized as a result of the parent's behavior, particularly if the parent exhibits bizarre psychotic symptoms. Children of depressives may also tend to be extremely sensitive to rejection.

Depression can also be linked to general medical conditions. Between 20 to 25 percent of individuals with general medical conditions such as diabetes, cancer, myocardial infarction or other cardiac conditions, or carcinomas and stroke will develop Major Depressive Disorder during the course of their general medical condition (DSM-IV-TR).

And Major Depressives have been shown to have a high prevalence (65 to 71 percent) of the most common chronic medical conditions (NIMH, 1999).

As we have discovered, severe, chronic stress depresses immune function. And immune dysfunction diminishes the body's capacity to fight diseases and disorders. Chronic or long-term activation of the body's stress response leads to what is called *allostatic load*, which is a prolonged wear-and-tear on the body. Allostatic load levels are high in depressed and anxious people. The impact of Allostatic load' levels on the human body can be compared to a car or appliance that has survived years of wear-and-tear.

Allostatic load is associated with impaired immunity, accelerated atherosclerosis, and increased incidence of type 2 diabetes, obesity, hypertension (high blood pressure), hyper-lipidemia (excess of fats in the blood). Allostatic load is also associated with osteoporosis (bone demineralization), due to its chronically high levels of havoc-wreaking cortisol and atrophy of nerve cells in the brain.

This stress load includes inflammatory chemicals like *cytokines*, which have a significant impact on behavior and emotion. Cytokines are a regulatory protein that is released by the cells of the immune system and acts as a mediator between cells when the body is generating an immune response.

Cytokines can both produce symptoms of depression

and depress the immune system. Depression occurs more frequently in those with immune disorders. Activation of the immune system induces sickness behavior such as apathy, lethargy, lack of motivation, and appetite dysregulation — all of which are interestingly also symptoms of depression. Some cytokines activate adrenaline-like brain substances and seroto-nergic systems (involving the brain's feel-good neurotransmit-ter serotonin) in ways that are similar to depressive symptoms.

Bipolar Disorder

There is no single cause of bipolar disorder. We do know that 80-90 percent of individuals with a bipolar disorder have a relative with either major depression or bipolar disorder, a statistic that implicates both nature and nurture. While some genetic ties have been established, the stress of growing up in an unstable home environment (e.g. with an untreated bipolar parent) can greatly increase the risk of developing a bipolar disorder.

One study shows that children of parents with bipolar disorder have an increased risk of having a bipolar spectrum disorder or any mood or anxiety disorder (10.6 percent vs. 0.8 percent). Children in families where both parents had bipolar disorders also were more likely than those in families containing one parent with bipolar disorder to develop the condition [28.6 percent vs. 9.9 percent] (Birmaher, 2009).

We're learning that no one gene is the sole culprit behind bipolar disorder. But so far, three "bipolar genes" have been implicated in some cases of bipolar disorder. University of Chicago researchers have traced increased susceptibility to bipolar disorder to two overlapping genes on chromosome 13: G30 and G72. This G72/G30 gene complex is believed to increase susceptibility to bipolar disorder by about 25 percent. These same genes, interestingly, are also believed to increase susceptibility to schizophrenia. So far, G72/G30 has no other known function. These two genes reside in a sort of "gene desert" near the end of the chromosome, with no other genes nearby (Gershon, Hattori & Liu, 2003).

One other gene has been implicated in bipolar disorder. In 2002, University College London researchers identified a gene linked to both depression and bipolar disorder: The Slynar gene, which is found on chromosome 12. The Slynar gene is normally found in the brain, but in people with bipolar disorder, the gene is believed to mutate and exert abnormal effects. This gene appears to be present in around 10 percent of bipolar disorder cases (Gurling, Mors & 2006).

Anxiety Disorders

Genes, environment, personality, and life experiences all play a role in the development of an anxiety disorder. We know that long-term exposure to major stressors such as abuse, violence, or poverty increases the risk of anxiety disorders. And genes, activated by stressful life experiences and certain personality traits, can predispose some people to anxiety. For example, people who have low self-esteem, poor coping skills, and a tendency toward neurosis or harm avoidance are more prone to anxiety. Conversely, an anxiety disorder that begins in childhood can itself damage self-esteem.

Anxiety disorders can run in families, and the propensity for developing them is believed to be influenced by the interaction of several genes. Like other complex psychological traits, fear and anxiety are influenced by many genes. There's no such thing as a single fear gene that lets anxiety spiral out of control if the gene's regulation is disturbed, which is what sometimes makes it difficult to identify the genetic roots of anxiety disorders.

But we do know some things. In addition to the 5-HT T and RGS2 genes previously discussed, several other genes have been implicated. For example, specific variations in the COMT gene, which regulates dopamine signaling, may play a role in causing anxiety and negative emotions. COMT encodes an enzyme that breaks down dopamine, weakening its signal. (COMT stands for a catabolic enzyme named catechol-O-methyltransferase.) COMTs two alleles are called Val158 and Met158. Roughly half the population carries one copy of each; the other half of the population is roughly divided between carrying two copies of Val158 and two copies of Met158.

Research suggests that people carrying two copies of the Met158 allele of the COMT gene may find it harder to regulate emotional arousal. This sensitivity may, in combination with other hereditary and environmental factors, make them more prone to anxiety disorders. The Met158 allele may elevate levels of circulating dopamine in the brain's limbic system, a set of structures that support memory, emotional arousal, and attention. More dopamine in the prefrontal cortex could result in an inflexible attentional focus on unpleasant stimuli — Met158 carriers can't tear themselves away from something that's arousing, even if it's bad (Hovatta, 2008).

Many studies are even showing strong genetic links to specific types of anxiety disorders, such as panic disorder, social phobias, or generalized anxiety disorder. For example, scientists are finding links between certain genes variants and specific anxiety disorders; variants in the gene ALAD, for instance, increase risk for social phobia, variants in the gene DYNLL2 increase risk for generalized anxiety disorder, and variants in the gene PSAP increase risk for panic disorder.

Most of the recent genetic research has focused on linking psychological disorders to gene variants that control neurotransmitters, but scientists at Salk Institute who studied the link between stress and 17 "anxiety genes" have made interesting discoveries about the role of enzymes in anxiety disorders. They also studied increased activity or over-expression of two enzymes — glyoxalase 1 and glutathione reductase, which are involved in oxidative stress metabolism. (Oxidative stress is characterized by the release of free radicals that cause cell degeneration.)

They discovered that increased activity of these two enzymes (which both humans and mice share) turns normally relaxed mice into Nervous Nellies and makes already-jittery mice even more anxiety-ridden. As with humans suffering from anxiety disorders, the sights and sounds of unfamiliar environments triggered panic in mice with anxious dispositions, causing them to freeze. And unlike their more relaxed contemporaries, the naturally nervous mice are not explorers and are wary of open spaces. Surprisingly, the researchers found that enzymes — not neurotransmitters — caused the high anxiety levels in almost half of the anxious mice (CITE).

Remember that many of us are slightly neurotic. Who among us hasn't double-checked to make sure that a door was locked or that a stove burner was turned off? But many of us have the capacity to turn neurotic, negative thinking into positive, hopeful thoughts. We actually have the capacity, through our thoughts and behaviors, to alter gene expression.

Attention-Deficit/Hyperactivity Disorder (AD/HD)

AD/HD is highly heritable; in fact, genes play a role in about 75 percent of AD/HD cases. Hyperactivity also appears to be primarily a genetic condition, although there is strong evidence to suggest that diet—including food allergies and vitamin or mineral deficiencies— holds great sway.

Many researchers believe that there's a malfunction with the neurotransmitter dopamine in people with AD/HD that causes an abnormally low arousal state, which causes people with AD/HD to seek constant environmental stimulation and activity. They create their own excitement and stimulation, if necessary, and have trouble self-moderating. What we do know is that the stimulant medications that boost dopamine function do appear to quiet symptoms for many children, as well as adults.

Researchers believe that the majority of AD/HD cases are caused by a combination of various genes, many of which affect dopamine transporters. For example, the 7-repeat variant of the dopamine D4 receptor gene is believed to account for about 30 percent of the genetic risk for AD/HD (Osher, Hamer & Benjamin, 1996).

SPECT scans have also revealed that people with AD/HD have reduced blood circulation (which indicates low neural activity), and a significantly higher concentration of dopamine transporters in the striatum, the part of the brain that's in charge of planning ahead.

What this genetic alphabet soup tells us is that AD/HD does not follow the traditional model of a genetic disease. It appears to be a complex interaction between genetic and environmental factors. All these genes may play a role, but so far, no single gene has been identified as the primary culprit behind AD/HD.

The Bottom Line

Genetic histories do identify risk factors, but having a genetic risk for a disorder or disease does *not* mean that that particular disorder or disease is inevitable. Behavior is always changeable, and is always affected by environment and experience.

The consensus is that genes are never totally to blame for our fortunes, good or bad. Large-scale surveys of gene-environment-interaction research suggest that only around one-fourth of the variation between the mental health status of different individuals is heritable, which means that *three-fourths is not* (Kendler & Baker, 2007). Each of us has plenty of opportunity to influence our circumstances and decide whether or not we will, in fact, become our parents.

AFTERWORD

The fields of clinical psychology and psychiatry exist specifi-
cally to help the emotionally unstable become more stable
and lead happier, healthier lives. Unlike in the eras of Vincent
Van Gogh and Abraham Lincoln, there is now professional help
available for those who suffer from emotional illness. Treatment
may require therapy or even medication, but hope is now available every single day in practically every city in the civilized world.

It is my hope that reading this book has been a transformative
process for you, and that your newfound knowledge of the human
psyche will guide you for the rest of your life in choosing stable,
rewarding relationships. Perhaps even more importantly, should
you discover that you or a loved-one show signs of emotional illness, you can move forward confidently to get the help that is
needed; and enjoy a more positive, happy, and productive life.

BIBLIOGRAPHY

Babcock, M. & Sabini, J. (1990). On Differentiating Embarrassment from Shame. *European Journal of Social Psychology, 20(2),* 151-169.

Beck, A. (1999). *Prisoners of Hate: The Cognitive Basis of Anger, Hostility, and Violence.* NY: Harper Collins.

Becker, J. R. (1981). Differential Treatment of Females and Males in Mathematics Classes. *Journal for Research in Mathematics Education, 12,* 40–53.

Birmaher R., Birmaher B., Axelson D., Monk K., Kalas C., Goldstein B., Hickey MB., Obreja M.,

Ehmann M., Iyengar S., Shamseddeen W., Kupfer D. & Brent D. (2009). Lifetime Psychiatric Disorders in School-aged Offspring of Parents With Bipolar Disorder: The Pittsburgh Bipolar Offspring Study. *Archives of General Psychiatry, 66(3),* 287.

Black, W.A. (1991). An Existential Approach to Self-Control in the Addictive Behaviors. In N. Healther, W. Miller & J. Greeley (Eds.), *Self Control and the Addictive Behaviors* (pp .262-279). Sydney, Australia: Maxwell-McMillan Publishing.

Bladt, C. (2002). The Relationships Among Affect Regulation, Self-esteem, Object Relations, and Binge Drinking Behavior in College Freshmen. *Dissertation Abstracts International, 62(7-B), 3367.*

Brickman, P., Coates, D.F. & Janoff-Bulman, R. (1978). Lottery Winners and Accident Victims: Is Happiness Relative? *Journal of Social and Personality Psychology, 36,* 917–927.

Cheng, H. & Furnham, A. (2004). Perceived Parental Rearing Style, Self-esteem and Self- Criticism as Predictors of Happiness. *Journal of Happiness Studies, 5(1),* 1-21.

Cheng, H., & Furnham, A. (2003). Personality, Self-esteem, and Demographic Predictions of Happiness and Depression. *Personality and Individual Differences, 34(6),* 921-942.

Choi J. Fauce, S. & Effros, R. Reduced Telomerase Activity in Human T Lymphocytes Exposed to Cortisol. *Brain, Behavior, and Immunity* 2008;22(4):600-5.

Cleckley, H. (2007). The Mask of Sanity: An Attempt to Clarify Some Issues About the So-Called Psychopathic Personality. *Journal of American Medicine, volume 17,* pages 101- 104.

Crossley, A. & Langdridge, D. (2005). Perceived Sources of Happiness: A Network Analysis. *Journal of Happiness Studies, 6(2),* 107-135.

Cummings, M. (2006). *Child Development.* IN: Notre Dame University.

Debecker, G. (1997). *The Gift of Fear: Survival Signals That Protect Us from Violence.* NY: Little, Brown and Company.

Diener E., Wolsic T. & Fujita. S. (1995). Physical Attractiveness and Subjective Wellbeing. *Journal of Personality and Social Psychology, 69,* 120-129.

Duberstein, P. (2008, September 24). Personality Can Hamper Physician's Assessment Of Depression. *Journal of General Internal Medicine, volume 51,* pages 17-24.

Ellis, A. (1975). *A Guide to Rational Living.* CA: Wilshire Book Company.

Emmons, G. & Diener, E. (1985). The Satisfaction With Life Scale. *Journal of Personality Assessment, 49,* 71-75.

Gershon, E., Hattori, E. & Liu, C. (2003). Functional Analysis of Genetic Variation. *American Journal of Human Genetics, volume 72* pages 40-51.

Goldman, D. (2008). Stress and Behavior. *Nature, volume 5,* pages 11-13.

Gurling, H. & Mors, O. (2006). Identification of the Slynar Gene. *American Journal of Psychiatry, volume 1* pages 73-75

Heimpel, S. (2005). Do People with Low Self-esteem Really Want to Feel Better? Self-esteem Differences in Motivation to Repair Negative Moods. *Dissertation Abstracts International, 65(10-B), 5403.*

Hertsgaard, D. (1984). Anxiety, Depression, and Hostility in Rural Women. *Psychology Rep.,*55:67

Holmes, T. & Rahe, R. (1967). Social Readjustment Rating Scale. *Journal of Psychosomatic Research, 11,* 214.

Holt-Lunstad, J., Birmingham, W. & Jones, B. (2008). Is There Something Unique about Marriage? The Relative Impact of Marital Status, Relationship Quality, and Network Social Support on Ambulatory Blood Pressure and Mental Health. *Annals of Behavioral Medicine, volume* 17, pages 12-14.

Horney, K. (1945). *Our Inner Conflicts.* NY: Norton.

Jussim, L. & Harber, K. D. (2005). Teacher Expectations and Self-Fulfilling Prophecies: Knowns and Unknowns, Resolved and Unresolved Controversies. *Personality and Social Psychology Review, 9(2),* 131–155.

Kendler, K.S. & Baker, J.H. (2007). Genetic Influences on Measures of the Environment: a systematic review. *Psychological Medicine, 37,* 615-626.

Kivimaki, M., Vahtera, J., & Elovainio, M. (Year). Optimism and Pessimism as Predictors of Change in Health After Death or Onset of Severe Illness in Family. *Health Psychology, 24(4),* pages 34-38.

Krueger, R., Hicks, B., & McGue, M. (2001). Altruism and Antisocial Behavior: Independent Tendencies, Unique Personality Correlates, Distinct Etiologies. *Psychological Science, 12(5),* 397-403.

Kubler-Ross, E. (1970). *On Death and Dying.* New York: Macmillan Company.

Lee, S. (1999). Body image, Self-esteem, and Compulsive Shopping Behavior Among Television Shoppers. *Dissertation Abstracts International, 59(10-B), 5621.*

Lieberman, D. (2007). *You Can Read Anyone.* NJ: Viter Press.

Loney, J. (1974). The Relationship Between Impulse Control and Self-esteem in School Children. *Psychology in the Schools, 11(4),* 462-466.

Maslow, A. H. (1943). A Theory of Human Motivation. *Psychological Review, 50(4),* 370-96.

Melville, K. (2002). Link Between Creative Genius And Mental Illness Established. Retrieved from www.scienceagogo. com/news/20020422222106data_trunc_sys.shtml

Nisbett, R. (2004). *The Geography of Thought: How Asians and Westerners Think Differently . . . and Why.* NY: Simon and Schuster.

Osher, Y., Hamer, D., & Benjamin, J. (1996). *USA Molecular Psychiatry* (Vol. 1, issue 5). NY: Nature Publishing Group.

Piliavin, J. & Hong-Wen, C. (1990). ALTRUISM: A Review of Recent Theory and Research. *Annual Review of Sociology*, *16(1)*, 27-65.

Pinkofsky, H.B. (1997). Mnemonics for DSM-IV Personality Disorders. *Psychiatric Serv.*, 48(9), 1197-8.

Ressler, R. (1992). *Whoever Fights Monsters*. NY: St. Martin's Press.

Rosenthal, R. (1976). *Experimenter Effects in Behavioral Research* (enlarged ed.). NY: Irvington Publishers, Inc.

Rosenthal, S. (2005). The Fine Line Between Confidence and Arrogance: Investigating the Relationship of Self-esteem to Narcissism. *Dissertation Abstracts International, 66(5-B), 2868.*

Ryan, D. (1983). Self-esteem: An Operational Definition and Ethical Analysis. *Journal of Psychology & Theology, 11(4),* 295-302.

Seligman, M. & Peterson, C. (2004). *Character Strengths and Virtues; A Handbook and Classification.* Oxford: American Psychological Association.

Sharma, S. & Rao, U. (1983). The Effects of Self-esteem, Test Anxiety and Intelligence on Academic Achievement of High School Girls. *Personality Study & Group Behaviour, 3(2),* 48 55.

Shrauger, S. & Rosenberg, S. (1970). Self-esteem and the Effects of Success and Failure Feedback on Performance. *Journal of Personality, 38(3)*, 404-417.

Suellentrop, C. (2001). A Real Number. *Slate.* Retrieved from http://www.slate.com/id/2060110/

Szasz, T. (1974). *The Myth of Mental Illness: Foundations of a Theory of Personal Conduct.* NY: Harper & Row.

Tangney, J. (2000). Humility: Theoretical perspectives, empirical findings and directions for future research. *Journal of Social & Clinical Psychology, 19(1),* 70-82.

Tassava, S. (2001). An Examination of Escape Theory in Relation to Binge Eating, Alcohol Abuse, and Suicidal Ideation. *Dissertation Abstracts International,* 61(7-B), 3864.

University of Toledo Police, Healthy Boundaries Program. Retrieved from http://www.utoledo.edu/depts/police/pdfs/Healthy_Boundaries.pdf

Waite, L. & Gallagher, M. (2000). *The Case for Marriage: Why Married People Are Healthier, Happier, and Better-Off Financially.* NY: Doubleday.

Watten, R. G., Vassend, D., Myhrer, T., & Syversen, J. L. (1997). Personality Factors and Somatic Symptoms. *European Journal of Personality, 11,* 57-68.

Wilcox, W., Waite, L., & Roberts, A. (2007). Research Brief No. 4. *Center for Marriage and Families, Institute for American Values, volume 7,* pages 22-24.

About the Author

DAVID J. LIEBERMAN, Ph.D., is an award-winning author and internationally recognized leader in the fields of human behavior and interpersonal relationships. Techniques based on his ten books, which have been translated into 24 languages and include two New York Times bestsellers, are used by governments, corporations, and mental health professionals in more than 25 countries. Dr. Lieberman's work has been featured in publications around the world, and he has appeared as a guest expert on more than 200 programs, such as: The Today Show, PBS, The O' Reilly Factor, NPR, and The View. Dr. Lieberman lectures and holds workshops around the country across a spectrum of fields and industries.

Contact:
Dr. David J. Lieberman
c/o Viter Press
1072 Madison Ave.
08701

Email DJLMedia@aol.com
Fax 772-619-7828

DAVID J. LIEBERMAN, Ph.D.

—YOU—
CAN READ
ANYONE

NEVER BE FOOLED, LIED TO,
OR TAKEN ADVANTAGE OF AGAIN

This work uses S.N.A.P – Strategic Non-invasive Analysis and Profile – a psychologically-based system that does not rely on body language, intuition, or guess-work. The Author's work is in use by the FBI, U.S. Military, and by professionals and governments in more than 25 countries.

New York Times
"Never Be Lied To Again"
and "Get Anyone To Do Anything"
Best Selling Author!

ISBN 978-0-978-63130-7

Have you ever wished you could peer into someone's mind to find out what he is really thinking? Now you can . . . **really**. This book is not a collection of recycled ideas about body language. It contains specific, proven psychological techniques that can be applied instantly to any person in just about any situation.

Dr. Lieberman has demonstrated the ease-of-use and accuracy of these techniques on hundreds of television and radio programs. In a special report for FOX News, host Jeff Rosin declared, "It's simply amazing! I was with him and he was never wrong . . . not even once. I even learned how to do it and that's saying something." In fact, Dr. Lieberman has gone 'head-to-head on live television, with skilled polygraph examiners and scored just as well—every time.

You Can Read Anyone shows step-by-step exactly how to tell what someone is thinking and feeling in real-life situations. For example, you will see precisely how to determine whether another poker player will stay in or fold, whether a salesperson is trustworthy, or whether or not a first date is going your way or the other way. And when the stakes are high—negotiations, interrogations, questions of abuse, theft, or fraud—learn how to find out who is out for you, and who is out to get you (or a loved one) and save yourself time, money, energy, and heartache.

Get your copy of
YOU CAN READ ANYONE
Available wherever books are sold

.